From Poverty, through Protest, to Progress and Prosperity

WILLIAM I. JONES SR.

ISBN: 978-1-4834-3735-4 (sc)
ISBN: 978-1-4834-3737-8 (hc)
ISBN: 978-1-4834-3736-1 (e)

Library of Congress Control Number: 2015914242

Lulu Publishing Services rev. date: 10/27/2015

DEDICATION

To my loving, dear wife, Geri.
Sharing our life and love along this journey for
over 50 years together is a blessing beyond words.
And to my beloved mother, Hattie. You are missed
with a longing too deep to express. Your faith in
me has kept me motivated and inspired on even the
darkest of days. I am sure you are smiling over
what you have instilled in me, and what I have
become as a testament to your will.

…Until we meet again.

CONTENTS

INTRODUCTION

DURING THE EIGHTEENTH AND nineteenth centuries, as well as through part of the twentieth century, Negroes were systematically excluded from American history by white historians. However, we contributed to that history through blood, sweat, and tears. Though under bondage, we contributed as laborers, on construction crews, as planters and harvesters, as crews aboard ships, as artisans and craftsmen, and yea, as fighters for freedom. Very little history was recorded about our value in the development of our nation. This exclusion was intentional by the white historian because the picture it created would have been contrary to the doctrine preached about the Negro.

My concern, and my reason for writing this autobiography, is that Negro historians are repeating the mistakes made by their white counterparts. The historians are ignoring the fact that now is the time to gather huge amounts of history about our race. A small amount is being recorded, but this is covering only the "talented tenth," or high-profile blacks. My personal concern is that there are a huge number of blacks still alive that could provide a wealth of historical material based on their lives. To me, a great effort should be made by black historians to interview many of our black servicemen from World War II, the Korean Conflict, Vietnam, and other recent wars. Many of the servicemen from one of our most interesting periods, World War II, are passing away without having their stories recorded about their trials and tribulations in a segregated military establishment. Our black historians should take their recording equipment and make a concerted effort to garner these stories before it's too late. The paucity of historical facts about blacks in history will continue unless this information is gathered and recorded.

Here is my story.

CHAPTER I

The Beginning of the Beguine

MY MOTHER AND FATHER, Hattie Rebecca Turner Jones and Joseph Jones Sr., were married in Bainbridge, Georgia, in 1923. This was his first marriage and her second. From my mother's first marriage, she had two daughters: Sadie and Josephine Randall. My father had one daughter, born out of wedlock, whose name I do not recall.

The Jones family moved to Albany, Georgia, in November 1924. They moved to Front Street in Albany and spent the next four years there prior to moving to East Albany. When Sadie, the oldest child, reached five years of age, she enrolled in Mercer Street Elementary School and later in Monroe Street Middle School. At home, she was learning and serving as a surrogate mother, cooking, washing, and ironing clothes, working as a family nanny at an early age. After Monroe Street School, she moved over to Madison High School, where she graduated in 1937. She married Samuel Davis Jr. the same year, and they both lived in his family home in Cordele, Georgia. They were blessed with a daughter named Mabel, and the marriage lasted approximately three years until they divorced. Sadie then remarried a man named Robert Williams, of Albany, Georgia, and they later moved to Washington, DC, for approximately six to nine months, later migrating to Chicago. Sadie worked as a practical nurse in the Cook County hospital, and Robert worked in a small firm making lamp parts. They both had five kids together, and all of them were girls.

I was born on Sunday, November 30, 1924 in Bainbridge, Georgia, at a small African-American hospital owned by Dr. Joseph Griffin. For a brief period of time, my mother and father lived with my grandparents, Florence and Andrew Turner, on the corner of Bruton and Campbell streets in Bainbridge, in the house that Mother grew up in. My grandfather was one of the few African-Americans in Bainbridge who owned a home and an automobile. He had acquired the property after he sustained an injury at his job at an ice factory in Bainbridge. Before the injury occurred, he worked in a boiler room. One day, while he was working, the boiler exploded just above his head, and the pressure blew off several of his fingers and his thumb on one hand.

When he received his compensation for the damage, he bought a home and a car. The car was a Buick Roadmaster, though he could not drive it; instead, the chauffeuring was done by his son, Willie. Even though my grandfather was not disabled in any other way, he decided he would retire permanently.

My grandfather, Andrew, had been a man about town and was now living with his third wife, Florence. She was also the stepmother who reared my mother, Hattie. Grandpa Turner was a very interesting character with a most unusual series of names. His name was John Joseph William Andrew Turner. Two of his three grandsons bear parts of his great name. Grandpa Turner's only brother was Thompson Turner. My mother's mother, whose name was Kizzie, was accidentally shot and killed long before I was born. Losing her mother at such a young age may have set the tone for the role my mother filled throughout her life. Mother was a model for all people that she met on her journey through life. She indeed was a very warm, sensitive, caring, and active mother. She talked very little about her early life, except to say that she was carefully nurtured by several people who were very close to her during her formative years. Those people included her grandmother, Carrie Turner, who lived to be over 100 years old; her father, Andrew; her

2

stepbrother, Willie; and her stepmother, Florence. In addition, there were a host of aunts, uncles, and cousins that influenced her as she was growing up.

My sisters, Sadie and Josephine, were daughters born to my mother and her first husband, whose last name was Randall. They were separated and divorced prior to 1922.

My sister Josephine was born February 21, 1921, in Bainbridge. She spent her life, from beginning to end, as the maverick in the family. From the time I was approximately five or six years old, I recognized that she was different, especially with her negative behavior. It was so negative that my parents sent her to live with my grandfather and his wife, Florence Turner. My parents received very little communication from my grandparents about Josephine and her behavior. She never finished high school and eventually returned to Albany. After living with the family for a year and a half, she got married. She had two boys, and after about two years, she went to Florida, where her boys became migrant workers. They traveled the eastern seaboard, from Florida to Maine, working the tobacco and vegetable farms. The family had little to no history of her life or her children's lives throughout the past fifty or more years. One of her sons, Robert, came to visit me once in Washington. Her final fifty years, until her death, were spent in Sodus, New York. She came to Albany for her final meeting with the family on July 5, 1976—the date of my father's funeral.

My sister Marietta was born on September 3, 1926, and her early years were uneventful. As she accepted her role as the fourth member of a growing, poverty-stricken family, her early growing-up years were completely programmed. Her primary activity was school, the same as it had been with her sister and brothers. She was well disciplined and receptive to learning and training. She graduated from high school, got a job, married, and had two boys named Marion and Leroy, and one girl named Betty. She later divorced and moved to Bethlehem, Pennsylvania, where she and her family presently reside with her children and grandchildren.

Joseph Jones Jr. was born June 3, 1928. Our life in poverty showed a consistent pattern at being poor but also having the ability to provide for a large family. Having a large family living on a farm was a plus for a farmer, but it was not so good for a poor, large, Afro-American family living in a small city in the southern United States. Several years after Joe was born, the political arena changed. Hoover, a Republican, was defeated by Franklin D. Roosevelt, a New Deal Democrat. We were still living in abject poverty, but a light was seen at the end of the tunnel.

Brother Joe's life was the same as that of other family members. Joe's school years were identical to his brothers' and sisters' school years: Mercer Avenue, Monroe Street Middle School, and Madison High School. Summers were spent on local farms doing day labor. We all spent part of the summer picking king cotton and harvesting Spanish peanuts. Joe, along with the rest of us, hit the cotton fields at sunup, having been driven there on a stake-body truck, and stayed on the fields till dusk. The cotton was weighed, and then we were paid for what we picked. Generally, the farmer expected young farmers to pick one hundred pounds of cotton per day, at the rate of one dollar per hundred pounds picked.

Joe took a page out of my book, so when he finished high school in 1945, he entered Albany State for one year and then went on to Morris Brown College in Atlanta, graduating in 1950. He then entered Northwestern University in Illinois, where he received a master's degree in science. He taught at St. Augustine College in North Carolina and then took a sabbatical for one year, during which time he got his PhD in science from Ohio State University. He later received a Fulbright scholarship to study in Ghana, Africa. After spending one year in Ghana, he came back to the United States and received an appointment at Texas Southern University.

My brother Thomas was the last child of the Jones family, born December 20, 1933. His brothers and sisters shouted in happiness and welcomed the bundle of joy. We all knew what he was facing, arriving in our state of poverty, with little hope for change and a bleak future;

however, he was welcomed with open arms. His route for life was laid out, just as those of his sisters and brothers had already been laid out. For the next decade, I was on hand to lead him to the "promise land." So I did, until he was ten years old, and then the country was actively engaged in World War II. I never got a chance to watch him grown up, as I was in the military, reaching for manhood and preparing for the development of a new country and a challenging new world order.

When my parents met, my father was a construction worker on river bridges in Bainbridge, Georgia. Soon after they were married, they departed from Bainbridge to his birthplace of Albany, Georgia. This marriage passed through some of the roughest times in the history of the young American nation. All of my siblings were born during the Great Depression, which was from the late 1920s to the late 1930s.

My mother had a sixth-grade education, but my father had none. I was fortunate to meet several of my grandparents on my mother's side of the family while they were still living. I never saw any of my father's parents because they were deceased before I was born. My father did have a large family of brothers and sisters. He was reared by his oldest sister, Marietta. His other brothers and sisters were William, Saul, Miles, Pinky, and Thomas. He continued to do construction work and other odd jobs. Working with his brother Miles, he learned butchering and cooking. He often did the butchering at local abattoirs for private individuals and groups. He and his brother were considered to be two of the finest pit-barbecue chefs in the state of Georgia. One of the primary reasons for that title is probably due to the fact that the pit was designed to allow the heat to cook the meat (e.g., pork or beef) at a slow pace rather than it being overcooked and burned due to the placement of the wood coal. The hog was cooked over an inground pit fired with both oak and ash coals to impart a certain flavor.

In addition, they prepared a special stew called Brunswick stew or barbecue hash. They were very proud and well renowned throughout the southern part of Georgia. They served high-profile groups at events such as political conventions and social gatherings. In addition, other dishes that they were famous for preparing were fried fish and barbecued chicken. When my uncle departed Albany and went to Valdosta, I became Daddy's able assistant, especially when we were killing and dressing the hogs prior to barbecuing.

When we first moved to Albany, we lived in a ghetto area that was not very far away from the city dump and not far from one of the very large cemeteries on the west side of town. Many of the people living in this ghetto area scavenged from the dump on a daily basis. Needless to say, the dump was the home of rats, mice, and vultures who were also scavenging. The only positive memory that I have of that area was the fact that in the house we lived in, we had electricity and indoor plumbing. My best guess is that we lived in that area for approximately four years.

We moved to the east side of town to an area called Sand Hill; it was so-named because of the quality of the sand present in the area. Removing the top layer of soil, we found beach-like white sand all over this area. This sand was used primarily to make cinderblocks and as a mixture in cement and concrete. The house that we moved into and four other houses in the immediate vicinity had belonged to a cinderblock manufacturing company. When we moved into the area, the cinderblock plant had been abandoned. The electricity had been cut off from all of these homes prior to our moving in. The water supply for these five houses came from a single, deep, well-water pump. The toilet facility was an outhouse—one for each two-house unit. Needless to say, during the summer, the stench was almost unbearable.

These homes were called "shotgun style," consisting of two units of three rooms each. Each family occupied a single unit. When we moved in, my personal family consisted of three girls, two boys, Mother, and Father. Mother and Father slept in one room, and the five children slept in the second room. The third room was the kitchen. The two bedrooms were heated using either a fireplace or a stove. The kitchen had a table, a large cupboard, and the cookstove. We spent most of our time around the kitchen table and in the kitchen area. For bathing purposes, we utilized tin tubs, primarily the number-three size. Water was heated in a large kettle on the woodstove, and the bathing area was usually the kitchen or one of the bedrooms. For lighting at night, we had kerosene lamps—one per room. The toilet facilities at night were called "chamber pots." These were made of porcelain with lids.

I was eight years old when our world shifted from total poverty to tolerable poverty. With the election of Franklin Delano Roosevelt, we could see some light at the end of the tunnel. He instituted programs under the National Recovery Act (NRA) that included the Works Progress Administration (WPA) and the Public Works Association (PWA). These humane federal programs, along with others, resounded throughout the country as lifesaving moves because concern for human welfare was the major focus, and the poor were the most visible recipients.

I recall that between the ages of eight and nine, I was aware of the impact of these programs because my father and I would travel to the city with my little, red wagon to bring the food home from the welfare warehouse. The quantity and the type of food given were based on the size of the family. By the time my brother Thomas had been born, my family consisted of six children and two adults, so we got a larger amount of food. Our allotment called for us to receive a twenty-four-pound sack of flour, several pounds of lard, margarine, cornmeal, grits, rice, canned beans and peas, canned beef, canned mutton, canned spinach and other canned vegetables, salt and pepper, soap, washing powder, and a large slab of salt-pork fatback. The welfare food was supplemented by our vegetable garden and fresh meat delivered by farmers, which included pork, beef, chickens, and sometimes wild animals such as deer, ducks, and rabbits that were shot by hunters.

My parents, especially my mother and her friends, would get together and design and make clothing. Some of the clothing was made from flour sacks and burlap bags. A special technique was required to prepare the burlap and flour sacks into clothing. For example, the bags and the flour sacks had to be bleached to remove the printing. We were the also recipients of a charitable donation of clothing given to us by the white families that my mother worked for. These items were usually dresses, pants, hats, and shoes that had been worn and required some repairs. Some of the clothing that we acquired was beyond repair, yet it was used anyway. We took those types of garments and cut them into squares, and they provided the basic materials for making quilts. Many of the women in the community would meet and have quilting bees. Sometimes, some of the quilts were sold for cash.

Much of the food was bought in cans or jars. We did not own a refrigerator or icebox for a number of years. Meat was bought and cooked to delay spoiling. We ate fresh or canned vegetables, and our bread was either cornbread or biscuits.

While living in this house over a number of years, we owned and kept a variety of animals. We had goats, pigs, chickens, cows, pigeons, ducks, and guineas. Our pets were dogs, cats, and an alligator that lived for about fifteen years. We often butchered a number of the edible animals: goats, chickens, pigs, and ducks. The chickens and ducks provided fresh eggs. Most of the milk derived from the cows was utilized in baking or for drinking.

My father was well known for doing the "unusual." For example, he would buy or build a wagon and teach the billy goats, utilizing harnesses, to pull the wagons while we enjoyed the ride. In his spare time, we would go fishing in the Flint River, which divided the eastern part from the western part of the city. I learned a lot from my father because I was the oldest son, and he was a hard-task master. He taught me gardening and animal husbandry. This was the general condition under which I survived for approximately eighteen years.

The neighbors were very friendly and loved and cared for one another. We were special to them due to my family's generosity when we acquired something that we could share with them. A good example was when my father went on one of his numerous cooking affairs. Often, he would bring back home several barrels of fresh-cooked barbecue or fried fish. Sometimes the hog killing, dressing, and barbecuing was done in the yard of our home. The cooking of the hogs was always done at night. So I stayed up all night, helping to cook and learning the techniques. The hog was cooked over an inground pit fired with both oak- and ash coals to impart a special flavor.

My father would prepare the food and supervise serving the huge crowds. Usually, after the party, my father would bring back hundreds of pounds of barbecue. My mother would distribute some to our eagerly awaiting neighbors. There were approximately twenty homes in our neighborhood that were the recipients of a gift of food. We were also very fortunate to be in an area that included an institution of higher learning, the Georgia Normal and Agricultural College. It was founded by an African-American named Joseph Winthrop Holley around the year 1903.

One of the special places where my neighbors socialized was the Union Baptist Church, which was located conveniently in the neighborhood. Typical of a small, Southern town, there were more than an adequate number of churches, primarily of the Baptist faith. The second most active faith was Methodist, which was divided between the AME (African Methodist Episcopal) and CME (Colored Methodist Episcopal). I do not recall an Afro-American Catholic church in Albany. Most of the Afro-American upper crust attended Mt. Zion Baptist Church. Union Baptist and Mt. Olivet Baptist were two of the largest churches east of the Flint River.

Throughout the city, Sunday was reserved for worshipping. All businesses except hotels, restaurants, and movie theaters were closed. Customs that were reserved for Sunday service were funerals and burials. In addition, baptisms were performed on Sunday. In Union Baptist, revival was carried out from the first to the end of July, with the baptizing performed in August. The Flint River, near the bridge, was the scene of our baptismal service each year. All of my sisters and brothers were required to attend Sunday school, Baptist Young People's Union (BYPU), and missionary service each Sunday.

Religion did not become a serious issue for me until I was approximately fifteen years old. Just prior to my fifteenth birthday, I was involved in a serious accident with an automobile while delivering groceries on my bike. All witnesses to the accident and the aftermath swore that I should've been killed. The car rolled over on top of the bike and me, and the only injury that I received was a broken leg with no other bruises or scratches.

Surviving the crash and the subsequent hospitalization and recuperation gave me time to ponder and question the "whys" of my survival. It was during that period that I realized that for some reason unknown to me, it wasn't my time to go, and that some power greater than me had spared my life—maybe because I still had a special purpose in life to be fulfilled later.

Less than a year later, in the Baptist faith, I accepted Jesus Christ as my Lord and Savior. From that day forward, I have accepted the belief that there is a power greater than all mankind who directs my life and all of my endeavors. Throughout life, I have moved with the feeling that everything I do is directed and will come out okay if I listen to my soft inner voice.

In college, I majored in science (biology and chemistry) and later worked in science for more than thirty years; however, nothing that I had experience changed my belief in God as the Supreme Being. If anything, everything I saw and experienced working in science only reinforced my religious beliefs. Science shows an orderliness that bespeaks of a control in and of the universe that even theories are inadequate to explain. Many scientific theories and treatises have been formulated to explain our existence; however, I find them inadequate in explaining all of the phenomena of all of our existence.

Probably the most fascinating is living in life itself—be it animal or plant. The fact that we have found only one planet in the whole universe capable of sustaining life as we know it gives the crowning touch to God's existence. We tend to revel in our ability to create, but in actuality, nothing is created or destroyed. Everything that we discovered is already here, waiting to be located and developed. I have learned to accept the fact that the hand of God is everywhere and that we are all God's children. For the aforementioned reasoning, I am able to accept and give full respect to all religious faiths.

CHAPTER II

Albany, Georgia: "The City"

ALBANY, GEORGIA IS LOCATED approximately 180 miles southwest of Atlanta, Georgia. It is located on the Flint River, which has its headwaters near Atlanta. When I grew up, Albany served as a rail center between Atlanta, Georgia, and Tampa, Florida. Albany was founded by Nelson Tift in 1836.

In the 1930s and 1940s, the population was approximately twenty-five thousand residents. More than 50 percent of the residents were African-American. Primarily, Albany serviced many of the farm communities from twenty to thirty miles around. That label was in evidence as one viewed the business community. The farmers brought their bountiful harvest of cotton, peanuts, pecans, sugarcane, corn, syrup, fruits, and vegetables. There were three cotton gins located in the town—one of which was black-owned. There were two mule and horse stables, one African-American-owned blacksmith business, four-plus auto dealerships, three supermarkets (Piggly Wiggly, A&P, and Rogers), two pharmacists, a JCPenney department store, Woolworth's, two five-and-dime stores, and several furniture stores.

The town had one hospital called Phoebe Putney Memorial, one white senior high school (Albany High School), one African-American senior high school (Madison High School), the Albany Cardinals baseball team and stadium, and four African-American-owned funeral homes. There was one white-only YMCA with a swimming pool, as well as two white theaters, one black theater, several banks, two pawnshops, several jewelry stores, and an African-American shoe-repair business. In town were also two bakery shops, one pecan factory, one major ice and coal plant, several pool parlors, and one hydroelectric dam that stretched across the Flint River. In addition, there were a number of restaurants, both white and African-American, but they were operated as separate facilities. There were other businesses, such as a candy-manufacturing business called Bob's Candy Kitchen, which is still operating today, a florist company, a baseball team, a taxi company, several barber and beauty shops, and a number of small grocery stores that were all owned by African-Americans.

Albany, Georgia, was also famous as a rail center. Trains that generally left places such as Atlanta and Macon traveled through Albany, Georgia, to Tampa, Florida, and other trains traveled to Waycross, Georgia, going to the east coast of Florida. Since most of these trains were coal-fired, they were serviced in Albany so that they could complete the trips to distant cities in Florida. Although the Flint River flowed from Atlanta to Apalachicola, Florida, the depth of the river and the rocky conditions did not allow it to function as a navigable waterway for large ships. The other method of transportation from city to city was provided by the Trailways Bus Corporation.

Afro-Americans had a wide variety of jobs that were usually characterized as "menial occupations." The jobs ranged from taxi drivers to barbers; cooks; waiters; busboys; gardeners; truck drivers; cotton, peanut, and fruit pickers; housemaids; construction workers; butchers; and other jobs in industries that required heavy labor operations. Certain jobs were considered as "top of the line" and were well sought after by Afro-Americans, such as federal mail carriers, railroaders, doctors, dentists, teachers, morticians, and ministers. The federal mail carriers and the railroaders' jobs were unique in that they offered good pay, fairly permanent job status, and good retirement benefits of the type that were typically unavailable to Afro-Americans in other endeavors. All of these jobs were filled by Afro-American men and overseen by white supervisors.

Afro-American women were expected to be available to serve in most of the white-family homes. The required services ranged from housekeeping, cooking, washing, and ironing to childrearing. Often, these women were transported to and from the whites' homes by their employers. Their day in the homes began at around 7:30 a.m. and ended at 5:00 p.m. Generally, if the maid/housekeeper was a quality worker, she might work for the same family for a long number of years.

The mayor of Albany, the city council, the sheriff's department, police department, fire department, jailors, prosecuting and defense attorneys, judges, school superintendent, and all city white-collar workers were Caucasian.

The courts and all of the so-called "justice system" were serviced by white justices and attorneys only. To the best of my knowledge, no African-American attorney was allowed to be a member of the bar, not only in Albany but also in the entire state of Georgia.

Ms Helen McBride
4950 Governors Dr Apt 1205
Forest Park GA 30297

CHAPTER III

Mother Dearest

My mother, Hattie Rebecca Turner, was born on June 10, 1897, in Dawson, Georgia, which is located in Terrell County. She was the first and only child of Andrew and Kizzie Turner – my grandparents. When I was born, my mother was approximately twenty-seven years old and had two daughters from previous marriage. The oldest, Sadie, was five years old, and Josephine was three.

Despite the fact that my mother had only attended school for approximately six years, she was a very intelligent, forthright, honest, God-fearing woman. She was a very talented person, with most of her skills displayed in her ability as a homemaker. Her educational background was fairly typical for blacks, and especially for young, black women of her era. She obtained a formal educational level to approximately sixth grade, and then she was off to work to serve the wealthy and not-so-wealthy whites. This occupation was a short straw that she drew, but she did not allow it to become a handicap as she journeyed through life. From that point in her life, she placed a high premium on education, and she attempted to instill that philosophy in all people that she encountered, especially her children.

Very early in my life, I recall her telling me, "Son, read as often as you can, and whatever you can find to read." She probably was not aware at the time of the meaning of one great writer's philosophy quoted several centuries before she was born: *"Reading maketh a full man, conference a ready man, and writing an exact man."*[1] To that end, she always brought home day-old copies of the *Albany Herald* local newspaper. On Sunday, we bought the *Atlanta Journal* or the *Atlanta Constitution* Sunday papers. This allowed us to keep abreast of local, state, and national news. To help me understand and acquire some business acumen, she helped me to become a newspaper salesman for the *Pittsburgh Courier* and the *Afro-American News Weekly*, which was and still is distributed nationwide. I also peddled the *Atlanta Journal* and *Constitution* Sunday editions. I ordered and sold the monthly addition of *Collier's* magazine. Because I sold newspapers, I was offered a great opportunity to do a lot of reading and to keep abreast of current events. To this day, I read something in my spare time. That reading habit has prepared me for my journey through life, and for her guidance, *I am now, and will always be, eternally grateful!*

She served a dual role as breadwinner and mother. I can still see her arising at the crack of dawn, going into the kitchen and preparing a breakfast of eggs, bacon, sausage, biscuits, grits, and coffee. The coffee was for Father and Mother only. The food was left warming on the oven for us to eat before going to school. For my mother, it was off to work as a domestic helper. She usually walked a couple of miles to the houses in which she labored, washing, cleaning, and cooking for her white employers. The return trip home was similar to the morning run, and her day had only begun. She usually would arrive home after we got home from school and we had performed several important chores.

She took in washing and ironing to supplement a meager salary from her domestic jobs (she was paid approximately three dollars a week for working five and a half days). Arriving home from school, we pumped and filled a barrel-shaped washtub and three tin tubs with

---

[1] Sir Francis Bacon. Quotation #2857 from Laura Moncur's Motivational Quotes. "The Quotations Page".

5 Aug 2009. <http://www.quotationspage.com>

water for washing and rinsing clothes. She scrubbed every article of clothing with Octagon soap. The white-cotton clothes and overalls were boiled in water laced with devil's pot-ash (lye). All clothes were subjected to three rinses and hung out to dry. In the meantime, she had the kitchen stove going for the preparation of supper. The usual bill of fare included a couple of vegetables, cornbread, and meat. She usually capped off an evening either ironing or sewing by kerosene lamp.

The only break that came during the week was her Wednesday-night prayer meetings that were held in various church members' homes. This involved a few hymns, a few prayers, a little business, and home again. Many of these services were held in the homes of members who were ill and could not attend church services. Money collected on these occasions was left to help the family. The only other break my mother took was to actually attend church service, to prepare Sunday dinner, and to rest, all in one day. As I listened to her pray, she always asked the Lord to allow her to live long enough to see all of her children out from under the feet of men. I think her prayer changed slightly as she grew older, and later, she wanted to live to see her great-great-great-grandchildren achieve that goal, and I would not have bet against it.

She lived through some trying times. Her second husband was bent on self-destruction through the "old devil," booze. She made a lasting Christian out of him after approximately fifteen years of nagging, pounding, and praying. When he finally got religion, he was one of the greatest Christians ever. If you had any doubts, you could just ask him.

This writing is in tribute to one of the greatest persons who ever lived, my mother. When she wasn't involved in things that I have already mentioned, she took on added responsibilities. Somewhere, and I may have lost count, there were ten or more relatives with a variety of terminal illnesses that she took inside her home and nurtured with care only a mother would give. These included her father, his wife, a number of her in-laws, her brother, her husband, and at least one daughter. In all of these cases, the person required many days, weeks, and months of individual and very personal care. Mother Hattie always rose to the task. All of the neighbors loved her, and many of the young and old referred to her as "Mother." She always offered a kind word, a prayer, and help if needed. She never needed to be asked to help; she volunteered. Whatever she acquired or possessed, she shared willingly. She would always find time to visit and minister to the sick and comfort those who needed to be comforted.

Her children were always seen as her pride and joy, and it also extended to all of their offspring. Although she had a schedule that would destroy the average mortal, if her children participated in any activity, she found time to sit in the audience and cheer louder than the rest of the audience. She always encouraged us to excel. Her aim was to put all of us through high school and through college, if we wanted to go. Five out of six of her children completed high school; two completed college and one completed a PhD. Her record continues with grandchildren who have college degrees. A number of her children pioneered in different areas, for which she is duly proud.

We speak of her involvement with her children and her grandchildren. I can also testify to her making a number of trips, some at great distances, to assist her daughters and daughters-in-law during the birth of their babies. She often spent several months at a time assisting with her newborn grandchildren, giving the type of assistance only a mother could provide. Her house has always been accepted as home by all of her offspring.

When my mother finished working in her employer's homes, she faced another series of challenges in her own home. One of the challenges was an extension of her continued obligations to her employers. In order to supplement her income from her daily occupation, she took in washing and ironing. We, the children, performed our jobs, which were to set the stage for the clothes-washing that our mother was to perform when she came home. The clothes-washing equipment consisted of one huge, wooden tub made by sawing a large, wooden barrel in half. A scrub board was designed for use with this tub. This represented the first stage of the clothes-washing.

17

The procedure required that we fill this tub half full of water and add washing powder and allow the first batch of clothing (white-colored clothing only) to soak for a period of time. Then the clothing would be scrubbed over a washboard and placed in the wash pot for boiling. Following the boiling of the clothing, the clothes would then be rinsed in three separate metal, size-three tubs of water treated with bluing that helped in the whitening process. The excess water was rung from each piece of clothing, and each item was hung on a clothesline to dry. All water had to be pumped and carried to the wash area. The washing of clothes was part of the chores carried out by each child as he or she became old enough to participate. We also learned how to starch certain clothing items, such as shirts that required starched collars and cuffs.

Some clothing that had been washed and dried received a process called ironing. At this juncture, it is worthy to note that most clothing that was subjected to this process was made from cotton. Irons used for ironing were metal made from steel that was heated on the wooden stove in front of the fireplace or in a charcoal-fired coal bucket. Starched items required special-care ironing so that no wrinkles were visible, especially in the collars or cuffs. Special folding techniques were used to prepare clothing prior to delivery.

The materials used in the washing of clothing were as follows: soap powder, soap, bluing, and lye. The lye was used when boiling only. It was often utilized primarily for dirty, oily, or heavy-duty work clothing.

We learned all about the process of making lye soap from our parents. The ingredients included tallow or kitchen grease from frying meat or other fatty materials. We used a cast-iron pot in which to cook the soap. The process was as follows: grease and oil were boiled in the pot. Then lye and water were added and cooked to a soapy consistency. The pot was then removed from the fire to allow the soap to cool. The soap was then sliced and stored for later use.

In addition to helping with the laundry, there were a myriad of chores for us to do. Each child was assigned to a series of chores. There were heavy chores for boys and much of the housework was left for the girls; however, we had to learn all of the chores, regardless of our gender. All of us were required to learn to wash and iron clothing, cook, sew, and clean the house.

My mother did all of the washing and ironing prior to our becoming old enough to help her with that chore. Often, after working outside of the house, she would be washing clothes or ironing late into the night. The work was very stressing because of the lack of modern equipment that could've been used in the washing and ironing processes. She was hampered not only by the lack of modern equipment, but also by the space necessary to work comfortably in.

My mother's church activity was generally dedicated to the second and fourth Sunday of every month. However, other church-related functions included certain evenings for missionary meetings held at members' homes. These would be evenings of singing and praying. Every year, in the summer, two weeks of evening singing and praying was held at the church, and it was called a "revival." Following the revival, and if there were converts, a sunrise baptism was convened on the banks of the Flint River. This was done in this manner prior to the church being able to build a pool inside. As I recapture the days of my youth and compare them to the laws and regulations of today, we would never have been allowed to baptize people in the Flint River because raw sewage from the city was dumped directly into it.

My mother's demand for us, in addition to attending school, was to attend church. So, early in my life, I remember trudging to Sunday school, followed by the Baptist Young People's Union and then evening service. If we attended the 3:00 p.m. service and/or the BYPU, we were allowed to miss the evening services. When we "got" religion and joined the church, we were expected to go to evening services. Those of us who could sing were expected to join the junior choir, and later, as adults, the senior choir. So the church was the center of our world.

My mother often spoke about her upbringing and how she was never given the opportunity to expand her horizon. She felt that if she had been encouraged to pursue an education, she could've excelled in school and in life; therefore, she taught us daily to put our best effort forward at all times. Since my mother had lectured me on the importance of reading, I was well schooled and aware of events both of a local and national level. I also learned some valuable lessons from interacting with people. I was encouraged to take on many odd jobs, such as working for farmers. In the summertime, this required us young people to rise early in the morning to meet the trucks that transported us as day laborers to harvest crops such as cotton and peanuts.

I recall that one started to work at sunup and continue to toil until sunset, with only an hour allocated for lunch and rest. The cotton and peanut fields were usually showing temperatures of over a hundred degrees during the summer months. At the end of the day, each person had his cotton weighed by the farmer, and he was paid at a rate of approximately one dollar per one hundred pounds of cotton picked. The biggest difference between peanut shaking and picking cotton was the amount of dirt and dust collected over your whole body and clothing at the end of the day. The only relief given was for a bathroom break (in the woods) or a short period to drink water. When picking cotton, you were allowed to work at your own pace because you were paid by the pound. However, peanut shaking was continuous movement because you were working by the day.

Approximately 95 percent or more of the farm laborers were Negroes, and the farm owners were Caucasians. Some of the farmers were very humane and gave breaks for cooling and water, while others were very strict, harsh, and mean. More than once while harvesting peanuts, I heard harsh words such as these: "I want you folk to bend your backs, and I don't want to see nothing but elbows and asses!" Interestingly, I cannot recall seeing anyone passing out or having heat stroke. I do remember seeing some of the older workers wrapping their heads in wet towels.

I realized, after a couple of summers, that farming was for the birds and sodbusters. So I abandoned the overalls, brogan shoes, and straw hats. My next working chapter began shortly after I purchased a bicycle to transport me to and from school and other engagements. I was approximately thirteen years old. Several supermarkets had opened in our town that rivaled the Piggly Wiggly—the forerunner of supermarkets. These two supermarkets were the A&P and Rogers. The type of service in these stores was not only unique; it also serviced most of the rural Saturday food shoppers. Several of us young bikers found a way to earn good money with some special entrepreneurial approaches.

Most of the grocery shoppers in our city did their shopping at these two new supermarkets. Since the town had no public transportation such as buses or streetcars and had only a few taxis, we bikers provided a unique and necessary service. Those who could afford it rode in taxis and owned cars. (The well-to-do African-Americans, such as preachers, teachers, postmen, railroaders, dentists, morticians, and doctors, owned cars.) Many people who shopped for groceries also wanted to spend some time in the department stores and therefore needed some way to have their groceries delivered home.

The bike boys worked out a deal with the store managers that would provide grocery delivery for customers. It worked in this manner: the manager of the store would give his official permission to approximately ten boys whom he knew well and were honest, upright, and trustworthy to serve as grocery boys to the store—unsalaried. The customers paid the bike boys personally to deliver their groceries to their home. The bike equipment had a unique design: a wooden ginger-ale crate was mounted on the handlebars of the bicycle using two metal horseshoes. The box was extended by adding extension planks and using ropes for securing bags. Often, this allowed a biker to carry two or more orders in one trip.

We, the bikers, established our customer list from people whom we met as regular grocery shoppers. When we met them at the store and they hired us to deliver their bags to their homes, they gave us their home addresses and keys to enter. When we delivered to the house, we were told to put the perishables (milk, eggs, butter, meat, etc.) in the refrigerator and then to lock the door and hide the key. We learned the routine well, we knew our city, and we were trusted to deliver. The store manager was gracious enough that when we broke any items, he would replace them for us free of charge. That was more than sixty-five years ago, and I still remember and appreciate Mr. Ragsdale, the manager. We would make between five and ten dollars a day, which was good money for the late 1930s and early 1940s. I continued my grocery-delivery job up until I graduated from high school and for a year after I entered college.

Black and White Confrontations

As I grew into my teenage years traveling over the city of Albany and surrounding counties, I had a few minor confrontations with my white "brothers." Typically, when they passed us as they rode the school buses and we walked to school, they taunted us by throwing objects at us through the windows; however, there were no injuries to us, except our bruised pride.

Once, a redneck was driving past me and intentionally drove through a puddle of water and splattered my freshly cleaned raincoat. He then proceeded to stop at a grocery store about a block away. I went into the store and bravely confronted him. He claimed it was unintentional and said he was sorry and gave me money to clean the coat, and was I surprised. I thanked him and left.

I sold Sunday papers on the east side of the river every Sunday. During one of the Sundays, a white boy, who also was hawking papers, saw me and claimed that I was encroaching on his territory and told me to abandon the area. When I refused, we had a short wrestling match, which was broken up by the white store manager whose store we were in front of. After that, I never saw him again, and I continued my Sunday sales in that area, because that was my home area also.

One night, I was heading home on my bike and saw four or five rednecks on the sidewalk. As I passed, they attempted to wrestle me off of the bike; however, I felt threatened and sped away to avoid them. They probably would have assaulted me if I hadn't ridden away quickly.

The last situation happened to my brother Tom and me in the middle of downtown Albany. I was in my army uniform, and we passed a couple of rednecks in front of one of the major "white-only" restaurants. These characters began to taunt us. So we followed them into the restaurant and dared them to come out and fight—but, no takers, so we left. Our move was rather stupid, because if a fight had ensued, we would've been jailed, because being white meant that they were always right—or so they thought!

These are some of the other jobs that I held after high school, before I was inducted into service:

1) An army airfield called Turner Airfield was being built during the early forties. A large percentage of the building program involved the laying of concrete runways for air service. These runways were approximately eight to ten inches thick. There were forms laid, with the interior of the forms containing steel mats and metal rebars. When I signed on to work, I was placed on the night shift. I was pleased with this assignment because it was much cooler working at night than in the extreme Georgia heat during the day. When I signed on, I was so small in stature that the supervisor in charge decided that I was too small for the heavy work of lifting steel and other materials. So, I was assigned as a water boy for the construction crew. My job required me to keep a bucket of ice water and paper cups at the ready for all of the thirsty workers.

Later, I performed other jobs, such as hauling and reinforcing steel rods and forms for the runway builders. Later, I was given a job of operating a mechanical cement vibrator used for removing air bubbles and spaces in the cement. I worked at the base from 4:00 p.m. until midnight and then went home to bed and off to school the next day.

This project was initiated to create an army-air force base for training combat pilots. It also lifted the economy in the southwest Georgia regions, as it brought a number of servicepeople and their spouses to the area. It also helped to provide good jobs to an increased population.

When the airfield was fully operational, we watched a lot of airplane activity over the city as the trainees prepared for war. I once observed two planes flying in formation that made a flying error that caused one plane to fly above the other, and they got hooked together and fell on vacant farmland. The pilot in the upper plane bailed out, while the lower plane pilot went down with the planes and was killed. Debris was scattered over a wide area. I also saw my first jet-powered airplane as it flew over our house. I was astonished to see this craft with no propellers and black smoke belching from twin engines. There was always something to be observed as we watched the Turner Air Force Base operations.

German POWs believed to be some of General Rommel's Elite Corps captives were housed at Turner Army Air Force Base (now Turner Airforce Base). They were often seen being transported in military trucks going to and from the base. None were ever reported as escapees.

2) I worked another night job during my youth at an animal-slaughtering and meat-packing company called Cudahy Packing Company. Animals that were slaughtered were pigs, cows, and sheep. The animals were driven into a chute, slaughtered, and skinned by special butchers that then placed the animals on an overhead moving device, where they were eviscerated by another group, washed, cleaned, and moved to cutting tables for processing. Prior to the cutting, the carcass was examined by agriculture meat inspectors and, if healthy, was placed in a

cold room for a period of time. The bodies were then moved to a cutting table for sectioning. The organs such as liver, kidney, brains, heart, spleen, tripe, and intestines, were carried to other areas for cleaning and processing.

I was given the assignment to clean and pack the chitterlings and place them in a container for shipping. Although this job was very dirty, and one which required a special device to remove the fecal matter, I attacked it with much zeal and fervor. The distasteful labor was forgotten at week's end when I got what, for me, was a fat check. It also introduced me to the world of craftsmanship. You were expected to purchase the proper tools for your trade. So early on, I purchased a special knife, a knife-sharpening whetstone, and a razor strop. I worked at a long, shallow sink with a special perforated rod for threading the intestines, and water was forced through the intestines to flush out the feces. Then the intestines were split open to finish the washing. I worked diligently because I knew that this job was only a means to the end.

3) By 1943, the US government had moved swiftly to gear up its production of weapons to include ships, planes, tanks, etc. Many of the young men waiting to be drafted in the military found work in war plants and shipyards. Shipbuilding was taking place in many areas throughout the United States near the ocean and waterways leading to the ocean.

I traveled from Albany to Brunswick, Georgia, to work in a shipyard operated by J. J. Jones Ship Builders. They were under contract to build liberty ships to be used for transporting military equipment and supplies to Europe. The US government provided lend-lease to the European countries. It was once stated that one to two ships were being floated from shipyards daily to be used for the war effort.

25

A buddy of mine, Mitt Wells, accompanied me to Brunswick, where we rented a room from an elderly couple. The room was co-occupied by two other young men who were also summer employees whose plans were to attend college. My father had also traveled to Brunswick to work in shipyards; however, he was housed with other, older men.

These were very interesting times for all of us. We were experiencing living in a world filled with anxiety. There was a war, and young men from eighteen to fathers who were forty were being drafted for service. Most citizens made every effort to adjust to wartimes. Many of us Americans had already survived the Great Depression of a decade past, and we were now trying to adjust to wartimes and more discomfort. We entered into this era, which found us faced with many shortages because certain items were being rationed. At the height of the war, more than thirteen million men and women were in the military, and the rationing was primarily a morale booster for the troops. Some items were actually and truly in short supply. Here is a list of some of the products: butter, eggs, meat, gasoline, milk, cars, tires, and articles of clothing, especially silk.

On this job, I was trained to be a chipper. The tool was shaped like a chisel and was powered by air. It was designed to remove burrs created by welding metal. This was followed by sanding until the metal surface was smooth. Summer in Brunswick, working on the job, in the sun, on and under metal surfaces, caused my job to be a very miserable undertaking. So I worked there for about a month. I enjoyed some of the community activities and a few spots famous for couples' dancing.

I recall one Sunday-night dance that lasted all night, and I still went to work the next day. Later, I took the train back to Albany, and the trip was quite memorable. Our day coaches had no air conditioning, and the only breeze came from the coach windows as the train smoked along. The trains were coal-fired steam engines, so soot and clinkers entered the coach as well as air. Typically, the coaches that were occupied by colored people were directly behind the steam engines. These provided the riders with the most uncomfortable conditions. The ride back home finished my short career in shipbuilding.

4) The main highway leading through Albany, Georgia, from Atlanta to Florida's west coast was Route 19. So, hotels and motels in and around town did a very brisk business daily, providing comfort for the white weary travelers. For a period of time, I worked doing a number of odd jobs at one of the Route 19 motels. It had a restaurant that served three meals a day to whites only. Their specialty was Southern fried chicken, to include a plate of fried chicken livers and giblets. During lunchtime and supper, I worked in the kitchen cleaning the dishes and doing other odd jobs assisting the chef.

They also kept a barn filled with chickens, and some of our work required killing, plucking, and cleaning the chickens that were sold in the restaurant. I also placed pitchers of ice in each motel unit every evening. Twice daily, I milked the cow, and she produced an adequate amount of milk for all of the uses in the restaurant. I worked this job for a few months during the summer.

My mother always traveled by a bus or a train, until she was approximately eighty years old. As a family, we got concerned about the length of time it took for her to travel using these modes and started to discuss with her a foreign mode of transportation called "air travel." She was not convinced and had a great fear about flying. I often teased her by using her religious beliefs about God taking care of her no matter what mode of transportation she was taking. I recall in jest in explaining to her that if she was flying five miles above the earth's surface and something developed and caused the plane to explode, that she would be better off because she now was nearer to God in heaven. However, she did not buy that analogy, so on her first trip by plane, Gerri, her daughter-in-law, flew to Albany, Georgia, and accompanied her on the plane back to Washington, DC.

After her first trip, we had a difficult time keeping her out of the air! She became acclimated to air travel, and it continued until the day she died. The only concessions made to her air travel was that after she turned ninety years old, we always requested that she would be loaded onto the plane using a wheelchair and also debark using a wheelchair to bring her to the curb, where the car was waiting. On one of these occasions, when the skycap rolled her from the airport to the car, when she was a block away from the car, she stopped the skycap, stood up, got out of the wheelchair, and walked to the car. The skycap was totally flabbergasted seeing her arise from the chair and walk to the car.

He said, "When the wheelchair was requested, I thought she couldn't walk."

I said to him, "Sir, when you reach her age, which is ninety-five-plus years, I hope you can move at her pace!"

The final long-distance trip that she made from Georgia to Washington, DC, when she was approximately ninety-five years old, she made by bus with other senior citizens. When she arrived in Alexandria at a Crystal City Hotel, I met her and asked her how the trip was. She said that she felt very good about the trip and enjoyed it with no problems whatsoever; however, she was concerned about a lot of the "old folks" who accompanied her on the trip. I chuckled because I was aware that it was highly unlikely that anyone on the trip was older than she was!

The greatest tribute to my dear mother was given to her on her 100th birthday, June 10, 1997, when the family secretly arranged a birthday party in her honor in Albany, Georgia, at the Municipal Airport Restaurant. Her birthday was a Saturday, and all of the participants arrived in Albany secretly on a Friday to attend her birthday party that Saturday afternoon. We closed it out by having a family meeting at the church and then dinner afterward on Sunday. All of the family members were pleased that we gave her this great party. She also appeared to be in great health.

Since I was the oldest of her children who was still alive, I took the position as my duty to give a special tribute to her on her 100th birthday at the gathering by the family and gave the following speech:

June 7, 1997

> *She was born as the only child of Andrew and Kissie Turner on June 10, 1897. At an early age in her life, she was deprived of the love and nurturing of a mother due to an unfortunate deadly incident. Kissie was the innocent victim of a hunter's shooting accident (killed instantly). Thus, this probably set the tone for her life as a survivor. She was reared in part by her father and two stepmothers. The most influential one was the last wife of her father, Florence Turner; however, she spent an inordinate amount of time with her grandmother, Carrie Turner, who also lived to be over one hundred years of age before passing in 1932.*

> *Most of her early life was spent in Bainbridge, where she attended school to a ripe age of about eleven or twelve. After that, it was working for others until she was well past eighty years of age. During those eighty years, she covered a lot of ground. Her first marriage, at approximately twenty years of age, produced two daughters: Sadie, born May 1, 1919, and Josephine, born February 21, 1921. An early divorce allowed her to meet and marry Joseph Jones in late 1922. Following the birth of her first son, William, she and Joe moved to Albany, Georgia, her husband's place of birth, in 1925. They were blessed with three more children: Marietta,*

born September 20, 1926; Joe Junior, born June 3, 1928; and Thomas, born December 20, 1933.

Her early upbringing molded a person whose life's philosophy developed into the character of a devout Christian, a sensitive person, a loving mother to her children and other people that she met. She has always been an honest, trustworthy, forgiving person. (I cannot add any more adjectives.)

I would describe her as one of God's greatest servants because she truly believes and trusts in God. Maybe this is why he has blessed her with a long life and us with her continued wisdom and guidance. I shall always remember her constant and daily prayer that God would allow her to live long enough to see her children grow up and not be footstools for anyone.

She taught values to live by. Her children were always encouraged to learn. She said: "Read, read, read—every day." And I have followed that message every day of my life and can testify that it was the best advice that I could've ever received. Using that philosophy, I have had success in many arenas where her admonition to read paid handsomely.

Though she worked days, nights, and weekends, somehow, she always reserved enough energy and time for her church services and children. Whenever her children were involved in activities in school or church, she was in the audience as the world's greatest cheerleader. She was a very proud parent who prayed of our success.

All of the children except one graduated from high school, two graduated from college, one with a PhD in science and one research scientist, one nurse, and two military servicemen. Her religious impact has had profound results. First, her wayward husband, whose major problem for her was drinking excessively; however, he drank only on the weekends. She harassed, cajoled, and prayed over him for approximately sixteen years before he allowed God to call him to duty, and we all gave thanks to God and to her for her perseverance and the change that came over our father due to her work on him.

I have often reflected on another side of my mother, which made her the unique person that she was and is. I have counted at least eight or more people whom she cared for through serious illnesses until their deaths. These persons she ministered to day, night, and weekends to service them with the type of care that was given only by paid professionals. Yet, it was all voluntary. These persons were relatives that were near and dear to her, such as her father, Andrew, Florence Turner, Mary Davis, Saul Jones, Willie Turner, Joe Jones, and Sadie. I am certain there were others too numerous to name. This, I must confess, was due to my not being around her for a number of years.

My own personal experience came two days before my fifteenth birthday. I received a broken leg and lay in a cast and was total immobile for over four months. During that time, I was helpless as a six-month-old baby. This meant that after her work, I took up the rest of her time. Only she and I know how much of her time was required in caring for me. I never heard her complain, and I remain, to this day, forever grateful.

As I reflect, I find it difficult to determine how she did all of these things that she did in a day, week after week. Her days usually began with her arising before daybreak to prepare breakfast for the family, getting all of the children ready for school and getting ready to clean, cook, wash, iron, and a myriad of chores for her employers. I had no idea how many of her "white folks'" children that she helped to rear. In addition, many of her employees were infirm, so extra care by her was required.

Often, she would arrive home at about 4:00 or 5:00 p.m. and would begin the second half of her day, which included preparing dinner for the family. Much of the time, she would begin to wash or iron clothes that were delivered to her home by the white folks. These were clothes from blue-collar workers, such as oily, muddy, and greasy work clothing. It required washing, boiling, rinsing, starching, drying, and ironing. Many nights, she did not get in bed before 12:00 to 1:00 a.m. One would have to see the crude equipment used by her. For an example, washtubs made from barrels, tin tubs, large iron pots, clotheslines, soap made by hand, irons heated on a wood stove or coal bucket, water drawn from a deep well pump, lights provided by kerosene lamps, and pot-bellied stoves. Needless to say, there was no inside plumbing for toilet facilities.

I failed to mention that most of her trips to and from work were done by foot. This was during the years when no buses or other location transportation services were available in Albany. No matter how much she worked during the week, Sunday was preserved for one whom she called, "The Master." Never did she lay her head on her pillow that she did not speak to the Master asking for his blessings and forgiveness. I vividly recall that when we were able to buy a used battery radio, her favorite program aired every Sunday morning from Cleveland, Ohio. It was an African-American gospel choir called "Wings Over Jordan" directed by Rev. Glenn T. Settle. This probably represented some of her most pleasant moments. Many times, I noticed tears as she attempted to get relief while she was listening to the choir.

She was and is a true matriarch. I am and will always be what I am because she was and is to me. I firmly believe that her indomitable spirit and all of her attributes account for the existence for all of us, her children. Her stamp is on every of us, her children, grandchildren, great-grandchildren, and so on and on.

She was touched by the hand of God as one of his chosen servants to do his bidding. She never complained, and it was always her belief that God would make a way. She loved her neighbors as God loved her. She shared her good fortunes with good neighbors, such as this scene: my father was an outstanding cook, primarily Southern barbeque and Brunswick stew. He barbequed for large conventions in our area, and he would bring home tubs of barbecue and fish fries. We would not be allowed to eat until she had us take packages of food to the neighbors (Ma Joe, who was very old, Mr. Tabe, who was blind, and other senior citizens and neighbors with kids). No one who was hungry was ever turned away from her door. I really cannot recall anyone that she viewed as an enemy. When business came to her house, church persons, including her pastors and friends, she rolled out the welcome mat.

My mother always showed great love for her family. Whenever we didn't call, she called and would never sign off without saying, "I love you." I'll never forget when I was in college and over twenty-five years old, I failed to write for a period of time. She promptly wrote to the dean of men, who called me in and read the "riot act." I did not forget anymore.

My wife and I were the recipients of the care that she reserved for family. Following the birth of each of our children, she came all the way to Washington, DC, to give her tender-loving care to Geri and the babies. I will always remember her trips because they were either by bus or train, more than 800 miles one way. At that time, she feared flying. When she was over eighty years old, she flew for the first time, and Geri accompanied her from Albany to Washington, DC. After that, we could never get her back on the ground. During the time of her fear, I told her that her flying should be ideal, because that put her closer to heaven; however, she bought no part of that statement.

I've only scratched the surface in expressing my adulation for someone who is by far the greatest mother in the world, and as long as she lives, she will always receive the best that I can give.

In less than a year, on February 25, 1998, I was called by my brother Tom, who has always lived in Albany, except for a short stint of a couple years while he was in the military stationed in South Korea.

Tom built his home, married, and lived with his children and grandchildren just a stone's throw away from Mother. We always felt comfortable about her care because he visited her almost every day, night, or weekend. He took care of her every need. Ironically, on the day of her untimely demise, Thomas was present as a witness to her final day of life on this earth. He was in the house when he became aware of her having some difficulty. When he arrived in her bedroom, where she was located, she was seized with a massive heart attack that met the end of her illustrious life on this earth. Many years before she passed, my brother Joe and I sent money to make her home life comfortable and give her many of the creature comforts; however, we never felt we could ever pay what we owed her for what she did for us from day one, with no hesitation.

CHAPTER IV

Elementary School Days

WE LIVED ON THE east side of town; however, all of the public schools were located on the west side of town, approximately two miles from our home. When I entered first grade, I walked with my oldest sisters to school. At that time, they were several grades ahead of me, and after a short period of time escorting me to school, because I was younger, they considered me as excessive baggage. So, I learned to go and come home from school with kids of my age. When my baby sister, Marietta, became school age, we accompanied each other to and from school.

I still remember each teacher in every grade that I attended:

- Grade 1: Ms. Brown
- Grade 2: Ms. Montgomery
- Grade 3: Ms. Dye (a substitute)
- Grade 4: Ms. Bertha
- Grade 5: Ms. Thomas
- Grade 6: Ms. Sprye
- Grade 7: Mrs. Holmes
- Grade 8: Ms. Wright
- Grade 9: Mr. Holmes
- Grade 10: Ms. Davis

- Grade 11: Ms. Sessions (All students in Albany graduated at the eleventh-grade level at that time.)

In elementary school (grades one through four), our mornings began with the students being lined up by class in front of the school building. One of the teachers played marching music on the piano as we entered the building and we marched to our individual homerooms, where we engaged in the morning period called "devotion." The devotion included singing Christian songs, reciting Bible verses and the Pledge of Allegiance to the American flag, and singing the National Anthem. The rooms were all heated by a potbellied, coal-burning stove in the middle of the room. My fourth-grade teacher, Ms. Bertha, had the greatest impact on my earlier years of education. She helped me to become an outstanding student in spelling. I was a good speller in her class because we often had spelling bees. The class was divided and stood along opposite walls, and the match lasted until one person was left standing. If you had to be excused to go to the restroom, you could not engage further upon your return. I had an embarrassing moment during one of these bees when I refused to go to the restroom and had an accident in front of all of my classmates. It was a great competition, and I enjoyed the challenge and learned to become an outstanding speller.

Elementary School Memories

There were a limited number of recreational activities for us at school. We had sliding boards, swings, and teeter-boards. Many of us boys wrestled to prove who was the unofficial school champion. During those years, there were very few fights on the school grounds. Usually, if you saw fights between kids, you would form a ring around the fighters and yell and root for your favorite. The teachers would often intervene and the fighter(s) faced the leather-belt punishment, and a note was sent to the parents for further action. Since the yards were not grassy but black dirt, we looked like miners after the recess period. If my clothes were torn, I faced stern chastisement at home. However, I would do the same thing the next day.

For lunch, I would have a biscuit sandwich from home in a brown paper bag. Most of the kids had lunch from home, or they would go to the local corner store for sandwiches, candy, and drinks. During my elementary days, we had no money for such use. A nickel or dime to spend on lunches was a luxury my parents could not afford; however, we never dwelt on our poverty, because we saw it as our way of life. Early in my life, I was aware that some kids had, and others had not. We really noticed these differences when we had rainy days or inclement weather. A few kids would be brought to school by their parents in automobiles and deposited in front of the school. Again, we could not afford such a luxury.

We traveled from east Albany to west Albany for school because there were no public schools on the eastside of the river for Afro-American children. It was approximately two miles from our home to the school building, which consisted of one small building and one large building, both grey wooden clapboard structures. All rooms were heated with a single potbellied, coal-burning stove that stood in the middle of the room. The walls in these rooms were bare except for a picture of our first president, George Washington, and several large chalkboards.

A separate building housed the bathroom, which was a large, open room with several commodes and urinals. The floors were concrete and were always wet. The elementary, middle, and high schools were within a few blocks of each other.

CHAPTER V

Middle School Days

My MIDDLE SCHOOL WAS located directly across the street from the elementary school. It consisted of grades five, six, and seven. The design of the buildings was similar to the structure in elementary school. It was a two-story, gray, wooden clapboard building, with each room being heated by a radiator. There were large, wall-to-wall chalkboards and a room full of desks and chairs. Again, the lavatory was a large, open room with several commodes and urinals, and these floors were also concrete and always wet. Privacy was an unknown commodity.

We were always made aware that we should honor our first president of the United States, George Washington, with a portrait of him in every classroom.

The playground consisted of a couple of metal sliding boards and swings similar to the ones in elementary school. During recess, we played dodgeball, jumped rope, and wrestled. Most of the students were well behaved, and there was only an occasional fight. If the teacher received a report about a fight, both combatants were punished physically and kept in the classroom during recess as punishment.

In fifth grade, Ms. Thomas taught us to be great readers, mainly because she had you stand before the class and read passages from books or articles. If you were unable to read correctly, mispronounced words, and didn't pause for punctuation, she made you stand in line in the back of the room and study the reading materials or book. If you were observed looking someplace other than at the book, she called you to the front of the room, where she seated you in a chair called the "electric chair," and she administered the whip—a leather strap across your back, and subsequently, you were sent back to continue your reading as instructed.

When I began seventh grade, I had difficulty solving math problems. I had also developed a bad habit of being five to ten minutes late arriving for Ms. Holmes's math class. So, each time I was late and she realized that I also did not have my homework problems ready to hand in, she sent me to the chalkboard to work the problems in front of the class. Needless to say, I had no clue as to how to work the problems that she gave me. After a short period of doodling and dawdling at the board, I felt her presence behind me in the form of a leather belt on my back and rear end. Mrs. Holmes continued these tactics daily until I learned to do my homework and to be on time to her class. Later in the year, I developed into one of her prized students.

CHAPTER VI

High School 'Daze'

I ENTERED EIGHTH GRADE in high school in September 1937. The first day was somewhat unique in that freshmen went through a hazing process as an initiation into high school. The exciting thing at the beginning of high school was that we were given a curriculum for each class for each day and we met new teachers; we had a real auditorium, and we changed classes each hour. My high school, Madison, was the only African-American public high school in Albany, Georgia. We did not have a cafeteria, a gymnasium, an athletic field, or a school band. Needless to say, we did not have an athletic program. There was no school-bus service provided for our students.

The school was physically located on the west side of the city, the part of the city where the well-to-do Negroes lived. Wealthy, by our standards, meant having a white-collar-type job, but not in city or state governments. As mentioned previously, well-to-do Negroes were employed as teachers, doctors, morticians, ministers, dentists, federal mail handlers, and railroad workers. The children from these families were often destined to attend colleges and universities and continue family traditions of success even in a segregated society. Some of these types were owners of small businesses. Interestingly, these families attended upscale churches, for the most part. There were very few churches of anything other than Baptist or Methodist faiths in my hometown. This was the first school that I attended that had a central heating system that had steam-heated radiators. It was also my first brick school building that I attended. Just as in the elementary and middle schools, we continued to receive used desks, books, and equipment handed down from the white public schools. The superintendent and all other school authority figures were white. However, our school principal and all teachers were Negroes. During the four years of high school, the basic courses leading to graduation were English literature, science, home economics for females and shop for males, history, algebra, geometry, and stenography for females. There were no courses in physical education, music, foreign language, or art.

During recess, we had pick-up games of basketball, football, and baseball. Most of the students would visit local stores in the area to buy their lunches. We had somewhat of an intramural boys and girls basketball team that played some games against other small town and county public schools; however, there weren't any league affiliates. Our basketball courts were clay courts located on the school grounds, so weather was always a factor. My hometown had mild weather most of the time because we were only approximately sixty miles from the Florida state line. I was ten years old when I first saw snow, and that snow was less than two inches and lasted for half of a day.

My second year in high school was spent at Hazzard Training School on the campus of Georgia Normal and Agricultural College (GNA). I ended up at Hazzard because a rumor was going around that students on the east side of the river would no longer be allowed to attend public schools on the west side. So, my parents and others paid for the private high-school training for me and my brothers and sisters.

My year at Hazzard was interesting because one thing that was added to my curriculum in ninth grade was music. I studied music under Professor Alexander Valentine, who was the music director for GNA College. Because the college had its own indigenous high school, high school band members were allowed to also play with the college band. I played the e-flat alto horn (mellophone) for several years. Then I took trumpet lessons for the rest of my high-school years and later, in college. Music opened a new vista to my life, and one of the most influential persons in my life was my music teacher. Music required one to be disciplined, to be focused, and to concentrate. It required much observation, especially of the conductor and changes in the music movements.

My instructor instilled confidence in his students to the point where we lost fear of making mistakes during performances. We traveled for concerts and marching appearances in parades. One of the most memorable parades I participated in was in Dawson, Georgia, at a farmer's festival where George Washington Carver, the renowned Negro scientist, was one of the principal speakers. The second most important parade was held in Albany for the city's centennial in 1936. The marching band also performed every year at the Christmas parade on Broad Street in Albany.

Mr. Valentine's reputation as a great music teacher traveled along the eastern seaboard, and many students from out of state attended GNAC to study under him. He could play every instrument in the band; however, his specialty was brass instruments. Several students left his class to become renowned jazz artists. Chief among those were Buster Bailey, a jazz clarinetist; Mack McKay, who played with the Dizzy Gillespie and Thelonius Monk bands; and June Motley, who was noted for playing two trumpets at one time.

In tenth grade, I returned to Madison High Public School. This school year, which began in the fall of 1939, would be a total disaster for me. It began on the thirtieth of November, my birthday, which was on a Saturday. It was my grocery-delivering workday. I was headed east at the intersection of Front and Broad Streets. I had the green light, but a Willis Knight (1923–1927 model) turned left into the intersection and struck my bike broadside. It was truly a miracle that I survived because the car's undercarriage was high enough to roll over both the bike and me. By some quirk, I crawled from beneath the car. Later, I observed that the bike was bent almost in half. When I crawled from beneath the car, I sat up, and my right foot and leg flopped over. I sustained no other visible injury.

Someone picked me up and carried me to the sidewalk, where I was transferred to an ambulance. The emergency vehicles at that time were regular hearses equipped with sirens. The African-Americans were serviced by African-American-driven hearses. Since there were no hospitals designated for Negroes, I was transported to the only hospital in the city, Phoebe Putney Memorial. The wards for housing us were segregated, as per Southern tradition. When my leg bone was set, I was in a plaster of Paris cast that was extended from the sole of my right foot to the middle of my chest. I remained in the hospital for a few days and then was sent home to allow the bone to knit back; however, after several weeks, I went back to the hospital, where X-rays revealed that the bone was not set correctly. I went back into surgery and the bone was separated and reset. A stainless-steel pin was inserted above the knee, and I was placed in a traction bed for several weeks.

The wardroom could serve approximately six to eight patients. This was the ward that was set aside for Negro men. In this room, I was in the company of two other patients, one of whom had suffered severe burns in a work-related accident. I smelled burned flesh the entire time I was in the hospital. In addition, his pain was so great that he was moaning in agony day and night. He told us how it happened. He was on a road-building and -repair crew that went early in the morning before daybreak to gas the trucks and prepare for the work of the day. It was dark, so they used kerosene lanterns to see how to gas up the vehicles. Some gas wasted on his clothing and the fumes reached the lantern, which exploded and set him on fire. He ran, and the flames spread over his body. Someone knocked him down and rolled out the flames, but the damage had been done.

Each day, the staff doctors would treat him by peeling and cutting away the dead skin. At that time, the technology for treating burns was very archaic. Generally, if the burns covered more than 50–60 percent of one's body, the chances of surviving were nil to none. He passed away several weeks after I left the hospital.

I was bedridden in a body cast on February 10, 1940, when the city faced a devastating tornado. The tornado cut a wide path across the city from southwest to northwest, killing eighteen people. Nothing in its path was spared. Homes, churches, schools, and businesses felt the brunt of the tornado. Everyone was affected by the tornado as it went across the middle of the business district of the town. It would require many years to erase the damage that was created in just a few short minutes. A short while after the tornado, I had to return to the hospital for the removal of the cast and more X-rays. I returned home for several months of rehab to regain my ability to walk and run again. I soon bought another bike, relearned to ride, and resumed my work.

Because it was well into the month of March and since in-home schooling, which would have allowed me to keep up with my studies, was not yet en vogue, I was out of school for the full year. When I went back to Madison, the school showed quite a bit of damage from the tornado. I continued to improve and started playing basketball and running track. I kept my affiliation with GNAC by playing in the band.

I continued to keep up with my studies and made the honor roll. I did not take any serious interest in young women; I never attended any of the social functions. Jukebox music was the craze, and some classes would hold dances at the school on Friday nights. The only dance I recall attending was the junior-senior prom. As a junior, we were required to sponsor the dance for the seniors. As I recall, my older sister taught me how to dance a couple days before the prom. The dances that we performed were the fox-trot, two-step, and the waltz, along with slow dragging and jitterbugging.

My senior year was pretty uneventful; however, there was one earth-shaking world event that was more devastating than a worldwide earthquake. It was the beginning of the Second World War, which came to our shores in the form of a sneak attack by the Japanese on December

7, 1941, on Pearl Harbor, Hawaii. After the attack, the United States declared war on Japan and Germany.

As strange as it may sound, there were thousands of enlisted black servicemen. I should thank God for the war because it changed our lives forever. Despite the hardships, opportunities were born. The entire country experienced a revolution of sorts. Despite the restrictions that were imposed on us when we were in the service, we traveled to distant continents, countries, and cities, met people of different races and cultures, and furthered the advancement and the development of a melting pot of the human masses. Many of these changes were experienced in foreign lands and whetted our appetites, creating a burning desire in us to make changes in the United States. Later, many of the civil-rights activities were born of a desire by ex-servicemen to make a change at home.

Some of the earlier pioneers had a great impact in setting the stage for Dr. Martin Luther King, Thurgood Marshall, and others. Mary McCloud Bethune, A. Phillip Randolph, Ralph Bunch, President and Mrs. Roosevelt, President Truman, and others were the cooks that stirred the "equality for all races" cauldron. Ms. Bethune and A. Phillip Randolph both served in an unofficial capacity to sensitize the First Lady and the president to the unfair and inhuman conditions that the black servicemen and women were being subjected to. They cited the discrimination, segregation, and racial intolerance being practiced against black servicepeople, even as they were engaged in freeing the world of tyrants like Hitler and Mussolini.

Although the beginning of the war made a change in all of our lives, we had to continue the journey that we had already begun. Therefore, I continued my studies. I had approximately five to six months to complete my high-school education.

In eleventh grade, I participated in track and got an opportunity in my senior year to attend a track meet at Tuskegee Institute in Alabama. The meet was an annual affair in which many Negro high school and colleges participated. Since most black colleges were in the southern states of the United States, it was an affair coveted by most of the high schools and colleges that had track programs. It was an exciting time for me because Tuskegee Institute was well known nationwide as the school founded by Booker T. Washington, a graduate of Hampton Institute in Virginia. In addition, it was the home base for world-renowned scientist George Washington Carver, who was still alive in 1942. One of the greatest thrills for me was seeing him on the veranda of his laboratory watering some of his plants.

In addition to seeing Dr. Carver, I saw one of the persons working the track meet who was an Olympic champ from the 1932 and 1936 Olympic games and Olympiad who ran with Jesse Owens. It was Ralph Metcalfe, who was a 100- and 200-meter champion sprinter. Later, I followed his career as he went into politics as an alderman in Chicago and later as a member of the US House of Representatives. This experience expanded my horizon and whetted my appetite to be a member of a college community and to get better educated.

Another sport that I had a minute role in was basketball. Because we had no gymnasium, during inclement weather, we ran practice plays in the school auditorium, which had no hoops. Most of the time, we played on the clay courts, but without the hoop-nets, except during regular games.

I accompanied the team for an away game at Americus, Georgia, which is now historically recognized as the home of the only US president from the state of Georgia, Jimmy Carter. We did not win, but I enjoyed this trip. This trip, like a few others, allowed me to explore other areas that I had never traveled to. Later, back at school, I took a role in our senior play because in addition to prom night, it was also a tradition for the senior class to select a play to be performed by a cast from the senior class.

My eleventh-grade homeroom teacher was very much interested in preparing her students for life after high school. So, she worked very hard as an interactive person to allow us to glimpse into a world heretofore unknown to us. This was the world of arts and humanities.

She recognized some of the talented students and was involved in trying to help students who were college bound to apply for scholarship programs.

I had many friends during my senior year, but I never allowed myself to engage in too much social activity that would interfere with my schoolwork. I never had a girlfriend, per se. And so, when it came to prom time, I had to go in search of a date and check with a friend, who loaned me his girlfriend for prom night. Following the prom, my homeroom teacher called me in and gave me some great news. I had been selected as the class member with the second-highest GPA and was required to be the salutatorian for the senior class. The salutatorian was given the honor to present the welcoming address for his class at the commencement ceremony. I think my mother was the proudest of all mothers that day. She even persuaded the wife of her employer, a judge's wife, to attend the affair. The ceremony was well received by all. I will forever remember the large crowd that was housed in the Regal Theater, which was the only Negro theater in Albany, Georgia.

In the summer of 1942, after graduation, my sister's boyfriend, Robert Williams, and I started on a journey to New York, by train, to seek our fortune. I didn't like the idea of going to such a large city. On the train, we met a young lady who told us about the opportunities in Washington DC and the many government jobs available. We listened to her and decided to stop in Washington.

I got a job working in the cafeteria as a busboy in one of the federal office buildings. My friend Robert also found employment, and we both worked five-day weeks. On our days off, we went sightseeing by taking the bus or streetcar, where we visited the major monuments throughout the city. We also visited special parks and spent a few days now and then with my Uncle Willie and his wife, Laura, who were living in Washington. I spent approximately three months working there, but I soon realized that one of my ambitions, which was to attend Howard University, was beyond my means to afford. Therefore, I returned home and enrolled in GNAC, now known as Albany State. I showed the magic touch on the entrance exam because I scored the second highest for my class.

Most of the students were from Georgia and Florida. The campus consisted of one male dorm, two female dorms, an administrative building, an elementary and high school, library, dining hall, the president's home, several faculty homes, and a huge building for classrooms and laboratories. For students, socializing was primarily done on Saturday and Sunday. The most noted area on the campus for socializing was in front of the oldest female dorm. The center of attraction here was a fenced area that held about six or seven large alligators. The inside of the fenced area featured a shallow, cement pool with an apron on which the alligators could sunbathe.

Some areas on the first level of the women's dorm were set aside for courting couples. All the males were required to vacate the building after several hours of socializing. Each dormitory was under the control of a matron who resided on the first level of each dorm. The males were always introduced by their girlfriends to the house matron during the social hour. When the time came for the males to vacate the building, she appeared and flicked the lights on and off, and the women escorted their fellows to the main exit. Curfews were rigidly enforced, and any violations might cause the couple to be expelled from school. The women were required to obtain permission from the dormitory matron, and they had to sign out and back in when going to and from the city. Some of the same conditions that were found prevalent in my high school were similar at this college. There was no gymnasium, no physical equipment; basketball was played on clay courts with no lights. Because the war was going on, we had no buses to transport us to other cities for games of any type. We played a few games with the servicemen from nearby Turner Army Airfield.

I met and dated my first girlfriend, Ruby Nell Hill, who lived on campus. She was a first-year student like I was. She was from Washington, Georgia, and we courted each other until I was drafted into the military in my second year.

The school held a program in the auditorium every Sunday afternoon. It was called a "vesper program." It was designed to showcase the students' talents, and periodically, there would be a guest artist or speaker. The college band would always perform, with solos being performed by band members or other students. It was a free concert that the public was allowed to enjoy. Following the vesper, it was social time at the gator pool or movies in the city.

CHAPTER VII

Military Induction & Beyond

By 1943, THE DRAFT age of eighteen to thirty-nine years had been set by Congress. I was drafted out of college at GNAC and reported to Fort Benning, Georgia, in November 1943. The process was well organized, but this was my first affair with the military. This was my first contact under circumstances that gave no one any privacy. It started with the physical examination through the barrack situation. It took two days for the processing, which included an Army General Classifications Test (AGCT), which was a type of testing similar to an intelligence test. Following the first stages of the processing, we were interviewed as individuals to determine whether we wanted to be members of the army, navy, or marines. The airforce was a part of the army at that time.

I chose to join the navy, as did two of my former schoolmates from Albany, C. B. King and Alan Miller. We were assigned to the Great Lakes Naval Training Center. A few weeks after being at Great Lakes, we arrived at the main center for processing. After more than sixty years, I still remember the misery of that day. Shortly after we arrived and got off of the buses, we were greeted by the ship's company, who were *cold* and methodical. In addition, we met the bone-cold, chilling winds coming off of the Great Lakes, and to make matters worse, shortly after our arrival, it started to snow. We stood in long lines waiting to be signed in and to receive a physical, billeting assignment, and navy clothes that were often ill fitting. Prior to all of that, we were sent through the showers, and our civvies (civilian clothes) were packed to be mailed home. Next came the bald haircuts. In some cases, individuals were sprayed with chemicals if they showed indications of body lice in the hair, on their heads, or in their bodily pubic hair. Other concerns were medical in nature, and our entry included dental and physical exams for visible signs of venereal disease or lesions of any nature.

Though we were to be US sailors in the US Navy, all men were assigned to their camps based on race, especially Negroes, as they were identified during that era. At the Great Lakes Naval Training Center, there were three boot camps for Negro sailors: Camp Robert Smalls, Camp Lawrence, and Camp Moffitt. I was assigned to Moffitt. My company commander was a third-class coxswain, equivalent to a buck-sergeant in the army. He was a tall, very stately, military-bearing person from New York City who possessed a "no-nonsense" attitude. He had the ultimate respect shown to him by his entire unit. He advised us that he was assigned to shepherd us through every phase of our training. We were given all of the rules by which we would abide. We were housed in a long barrack with two levels. Bunk beds were two levels.

We were given two white, canvas bags. The largest one was called a "sea-bag," and it was approximately 3–4 feet long and 18–20 inches in diameter. These bags stored all of our clothing and personal belongings. We were taught the navy method of folding and tying the clothing so that it would all fit in the sea-bag, including our boots and leggings. These two bags were strapped on a pipe stanchion behind the individual's bunk bed. Each floor had a washroom with sinks and scrub boards with octagon soap. Next to the washroom was a room that was heated to dry clothing over night. With the navy, cleanliness was next to godliness, so we washed and dried all personal clothing and bedding. There were a myriad of rules and regulations that we followed, such as reveille at five a.m. and lights out at ten p.m. The bugle calls dictated that. We could smoke only when the smoking light was on. We went to the mess hall, drill hall, movies, and all other activities together. Some of the other activities were drilling, swimming classes, knot-tying classes, and other training sessions as required. The only day that we had to lounge and take it easy was Sunday.

Because of the severe weather in the Great Lakes area, all of our activities were indoors, primarily in large armories. I was a trumpet player, so soon after I got to my boot camp, I was allowed to join the Drum and Bugle Corps. I played reveille and taps each day, so I was exempt from other activities such as KP (kitchen police), latrine duty, and policing the grounds. The boot camp ended after about eight weeks, and we were all dispatched to our first leave, which was two weeks long. I went back to my home in Albany, and since it was the spring break for the colleges, all of the students, including my girlfriend, Ruby, were on their spring break. I decided to go to her hometown to visit her. So, I boarded the bus and went to Washington, Georgia.

While traveling to Washington, Georgia, I went through a couple of small, redneck Georgia towns. We had a layover in one of the small towns in northeast Georgia leading to Washington. As usual, we were told that we had a few minutes' layover and we were expected to go into the bus station, relax, and await the call for the continuation of the trip. While I was traveling, I purposefully wore my navy uniform. Knowing the racial attitude of the Southern rednecks, I felt that they would have more respect for a serviceman and patriotic feeling toward a service-uniformed Negro over and above their feelings for any civilian. My calculations of that attitude proved to be in error.

After leaving the bus and going inside of the waiting area, I saw the usual lousy facility designated for Negro passengers. Negroes generally described this as being the worst of "fleabag" conditions. It was dirty and unkempt, crowded, and smelly. In addition, there was a small cubbyhole where you could order food and drink—if they felt that they had time to serve you. Seeing all of this, and wanting clean, fresh air, I decided I would wait outside of the bus station for the arrival of the bus. A short, pudgy redneck constable on duty at the bus station took it upon himself to confront me, demanding that I go back to the inside and stay until the bus arrived. When I indicated that I preferred being in the open air, he placed his hand on his weapon and said, "I want you to go back to the inside." So, I went and remained inside until the bus arrived.

I spent a couple of days with Ruby at her house and met all of her family members and friends. When my visit was completed, I went back to Albany to spend a few more days. The trip to Washington, Georgia, ended my relationship with Ruby. I then went back to camp in Great Lakes, Illinois. Near the end of my boot camp, I contacted a severe case of laryngitis that lasted a few weeks after I completed my boot-camp furlough. After the furlough, I came back to camp for a permanent assignment and further training. My base assignment was at the Great Lakes Naval Medical Corpsmen School. The training lasted for eight weeks and was to prepare us to be medical technicians on the battlefield, treating wounded service personnel. During school time, we learned to dress wounds, give medication, and serve as nurses under the control of the nurses who were solely in charge of the wards. In addition to patient care, the corpsmen were also responsible for preparing the work details needed in the wards.

There was nothing remarkable or highly exciting at the training facility. When we received our certificates, we were assigned to hospitals throughout the country; however, Negroes were not assigned to ships or to the battlefield while I was in the corps. So, many of us remained on duty at the main hospital, which was receiving white marines and sailors from the Pacific theater. Being at the hospital meant 8:00 a.m. to 4:00 p.m. duty and rotating to night shifts, which were occasionally from 4:00 p.m. to midnight and from midnight to 8:00 a.m. The interesting thing was that the Negro corpsman worked with, recreated with, and ate with the Caucasians but had separate sleeping facilities. Two of the main jobs that were most critical were dispensing medications and medical record-keeping. After gaining a certain amount of experience, corpsmen were assigned to cover a full ward of patients that required independence and responsibility.

The work required an eight-hour shift of duty, which, after awhile, was boring and tedious. Many of the unmarried corpsmen were hoping to be shipped out to see more action; however, because of the policies that were in place, especially in the navy service, Negroes were kept from front-line activities.

Shortly before I entered the navy, Negroes were steward mates and cooks. Once the seaman ship branch was open to Negroes, we trained, but aboard-ship duties were often not in our future. The white public and servicemen saw this as necessary mainly because ship quarters were cramped and there was no desire to have any close contact with Negroes. Throughout the lives of most Caucasians, they thought that being in close contact with Negroes was illegal, immoral, and downright disgusting because of their perceived unsanitary and unhealthy lifestyles. The propaganda received by whites about Negroes was second only to the propaganda issued by Hitler and his cronies about Jewish people. Under these conditions, the policy of keeping Negroes separated because of their race was similar to their treatment in civilian life and was prevalent throughout the theaters of war.

I was affected by my station assignments and jobs to be performed. This was my lot, so I never went aboard a ship during my two and a half years of navy duty. This act by the American government and the navy probably saved my life. A large percentage of navy corpsmen were attached to the marines, who were doing a great job during the Pacific theater of the war. Much of the fighting in the Pacific was called "island hopping." The strikes were quick and often of short duration, which suited the marines' style and type of engagement. A large number of corpsmen performed duties with the marines, but no Negroes that I am aware of. Most of the Negro corpsmen received only stateside duty. While I was working at Great Lakes, most of the patients were white marines from the Pacific theater. Most of the wounds were from shrapnel. Navy corpsmen on the battlefield primarily served the marines in combat.

When we were off duty, we spent much of our time in Chicago. It was a great city for servicemen. The USO (United Service Organization) facility provided a home away from home: food, shelter, and entertainment. There was professional baseball, football, hockey, and movies—all free. All public transportation for servicemen was free. The city also had great jitney and taxi service. Chicago was very strict about underage drinking. So, servicemen under the age of twenty-one weren't allowed in bars. Therefore, I was in the age group that was excluded from nightclubs and bars.

The USO that I frequented was on the south side of Chicago, where most of the Negroes lived. Most of the activity at the USO was on Saturday night and Sunday afternoon meeting young women, dancing, and enjoying their companionship. The women, who were the hostesses and were members of the USO, were not allowed to fraternize with a serviceman after their tours at the USO. Often, big bands such as Ellington, Basie, Hampton, and others played at the Regal Theater on the south side, and we attended these concerts. Periodically, we would frequent the Lake Michigan beaches near downtown Chicago. The young servicemen participated in all of the very wholesome activities— primarily because their choices were limited.

I had relatives, an uncle and my sister and her family, whom I often visited. Approximately one year after serving at the main hospital, I requested to be trained as a medical technologist, and I was transferred to the Bethesda Navy Medical Center for training. The course lasted for four months, and then I was transferred for duty to the Naval Technical Training Center in Millington, Tennessee. While I was at Bethesda, I spent most of my liberty time near the U-Street area of DC. I was not familiar with any USO services in DC.

During my four-month tour of duty at Bethesda, I met one Afro-American naval patient, who traveled with me to DC. I now remember this person because of a very hair-raising experience I had with him while traveling from Bethesda to Washington, DC. The public buses in Maryland carried passengers heading to DC to the streetcar line at Wisconsin and Western Avenue. On the Maryland side of Wisconsin Avenue, there was a snack-food restaurant where we could get a snack while waiting for the trolley. He and I went to the counter and ordered food, and when we received it, we proceeded to eat. The lady at the counter explained to us that we couldn't eat in the restaurant and we would have to go outside and eat while we waited for the trolley. When my buddy heard that, he went into a rage; he was very irritated and began cursing. He was not going to accept that type of treatment after being in combat and risking his life for this, as he said, *"Goddamn, motherfucking racist country!"*

His next move shocked everyone—including me—because he approached the food and drink on the counter and, with a very emphatic wave of his hand, pushed everything off of the counter and onto the floor. Then he and I walked out of the door. For the next ten minutes or so, we waited for the streetcar outside, and I kept watching for the arrival of the Montgomery County Police, but they never came. Even as we boarded the streetcar and traveled into DC, I still expected to see the cops following us.

Following four months at Bethesda, I was shipped to Millington, Tennessee, to start a new chapter in my naval saga. The trip to Tennessee was made by train and required approximately twenty-four hours of travel. During the first twelve hours, my fellow shipmates and I traveled in style by Pullman sleeping cars. The racial make-up of the contingent was nine Caucasians and one Negro—me. There was no problem aboard as we traveled that night and into the morning when we arrived in Chattanooga, Tennessee. There, we were required to change trains to a day coach, and then we were on our way to Memphis.

We debarked from the Pullman coach to enter the day coach. Our senior NCO (non-commissioned officer) had the tickets and presented them to the conductor for our boarding. I was in line just in front of the senior NCO. As I approached the train conductor, he gestured for me to enter the Negro, or colored, coach. My NCO stepped in front of me and told the conductor that all of us were required to ride together in the same coach to which we were assigned. The conductor argued that the states controlled the seating, and even though we were in the military, we would abide by state's rules. My NCO told him he was responsible for the whole contingent and he would not accept separation of any member from the group. The argument was waged for several tense minutes. During this period, I was very concerned because I was aware of the state laws and of the zeal of groups such as the confederate Ku Klux Klan, their attitudes, actions, and of most southerners at that time. The attitude of many Negroes in the South, who were wholly aware of fighting against the system, was to keep a low profile because you had a no-win situation; therefore, I stood off to the side while the argument ensued over where I was to be located.

The conductor told my NCO that if the situation was not resolved in three minutes, he was ordering the train to pull off and leave us standing. The NCO apprised the conductor of the illegality of his position. It went thusly: during wartime, all transportation in the United States was under the control of the Department of the Army, and he would call the federal department and have troops intercept the train to enforce the law. In addition, he ensured the conductor that anyone who interfered with or obstructed troop movement, which would include him, would be jailed. The conductor finally relented, and I traveled to Memphis in the all-white coach. He relented with a special warning and advice that I would be seated with my group at all times. Most of the white passengers viewed the situation in utter disbelief.

The second half of this situation was played out as we went to the dining car for breakfast, and later, for lunch. Each time, my mates and I lined up with me being placed in the middle of the lineup, and we proceeded to sit in the white-only section of the dining car. The custom during that time was separation in the dining car by isolating two to four tables using curtains for cordoning off the area for Negroes. Nothing untoward happened throughout the trip except that the conductor later saw us engaging in a penny anti-poker game and threatened to throw us off of the train if we did not desist. He told us that gambling was unlawful in the state of Tennessee and aboard his train in that state. This incident has so far been unrecorded except in my memory and that of the other sailors who were affected. We debarked at the Memphis, Tennessee, train station, where our military transportation awaited.

Being stationed near Memphis brought me into a new world, the likes of which I had never experienced before or since. This city was the place where the blues was born; it was the home place of W. C. Handy, the great cornetist that wrote and popularized the blues. His two most popular songs were "Saint Louis Blues" and "Memphis Blues." The city of Memphis is home to Beale Street, one of the most well-known streets in the world. I saw W. C. Handy in a parade on Beale Street in 1945. I classify that as one of my greatest thrills. The fact that the war was in full swing and there was a huge shortage of men meant that most servicemen felt that being in Memphis was like dying and going to heaven. This was primarily due to the huge number of very beautiful women who needed and wanted to be entertained. Unlike in Chicago, there were no restrictions meted out against underage servicemen. However, there was another town nearby, West Memphis, which was across the Mississippi River in Arkansas, which was truly open to anything, including gambling.

When I arrived on the base located at Millington, Tennessee, which was approximately twenty miles outside of Memphis, I was greeted with the usual on-base housing arrangements. The big difference there was that there was no separation of personnel in the Negro barracks. For example, we were not housed according to military-operation specialties. I was the first school-trained hospital corpsman to arrive for duty at the Naval Aviation Air Technical Training Center (NAATTC) Base. I was assigned to work in one of the medical dispensaries. The dispensary contained two wards: one for the Negro sailors and the other for "Caucasoids" (AKA rednecks). I was required to minister to the Negro sailors only. My daily routine included giving medications and other physician-ordered treatments to the sailors. One of the most important parts of this job was medical record-keeping. The sailors being treated were expected to return to duty after treatment, or for a short term of less than two weeks. If longer treatment and medication were required, they would be transferred to the naval hospital at Millington.

For about a year, this was my daily routine between 9:00 a.m. and 5:00 p.m. There were a few recreation centers on the base for our use; however, most of us were ready to spend much of our time off base in Memphis. Sometimes, when we stayed on base, we played card games, such as bridge, pinochle, blackjack, or poker, and other games in the barracks. My favorite card game was poker, in which we gambled with some of our hard-earned paychecks. We always kept enough in reserve for our journeys to the city to spend on its offerings. Most of my trips were made to the Memphis USO Center, which provided food, shelter, and entertainment free to the servicemen. The social entertainment provided by the USO allowed many of us to meet some of the top-of-the-line Memphis belles.

After a short period of time, I became acquainted with a beautiful, young, high-school girl, whom I courted for more than four years. Her name was Opal Lee Taylor. Her immediate family consisted of one brother and one sister who lived in Chicago. So, after awhile, most of my trips into Memphis ended at her home. We attended many social functions together. Although she was my main girlfriend, I did not ignore the attention of some of the other young women. We were all aware that the uniform attracted the attention of many young women. We made no attempt to back away from their adulation.

During my stay in Millington, I traveled a lot with one of my medical associates who became my nearest and dearest friend. His name was Julian McConnell, and he was from Washington, DC. He was a medic that received base training and worked as a lab technician. He was older than I, and he became my mentor for socializing. He was handsome, socially inclined, intelligent, and most of all, a lothario. I learned well! When I was discharged from the navy, I did not forget that my life's goals were still to be accomplished. My first goal was to go back to college and establish a lifetime career. Because I had worked in the medical field, I envisioned medicine as a chosen career. To that end, I applied to three colleges for admission. They were: Morehouse College in Atlanta, Georgia; Tuskegee Institute in Tuskegee, Alabama; and Hampton Institute in Hampton, Virginia.

Having served in the military in and around Chicago, I decided that I would go there to get a job and prepare for my college career. The reason for my selecting Chicago was the fact that I had relatives there. My sister Sadie and my uncle, Willie Turner, were both living in the same apartment on the south side of Chicago.

When I arrived in Chicago, I didn't realize how difficult it would be for me, as a Negro, to find basic employment. I first looked in the newspaper classified ads for jobs that were basically assigned to Negroes; however, I found that the unions controlled. Caucasians of foreign nationalities held many of these jobs.

My brother-in-law and uncle were both working on the west side of Chicago in a small factory making lamp parts. These parts were metal used in ceiling and table lamps. The owner was a Hungarian immigrant who practiced equal-employment opportunities. I accompanied them to work, met the owner, and requested employment. His first statement was that he was interested in hiring full-time employees, and he asked if I would be a full-time employee. I hesitated for a period while examining my conscience for an answer. Finally, I leveled with him. I told him that I planned to work only during the summer and that my goal was to then go to college. My first inclination, spurred by a conversation that I'd had earlier with my brother-in-law, was to state to the employer that I was seeking full-time work. My brother-in-law assured me that if I gave the wrong answer, I probably would not be hired. I was surprised by what happened after I told the truth about my intentions. The owner and employer, Mr. Dack, indicated that he was most impressed by my answer.

He said, "Young man, you are hired because I feel that I will be doing something for you to enhance your career, and would be proud to see you take that step." In addition, he said, "Because you were truthful, I stand ready to have you come back every summer while you're in college, and a job will be ready here for you."

So, in that instance, my summer career was established, and I followed through every year.

In January 1947, I boarded a train for Hampton Institute. When I arrived from Chicago into Washington DC, I changed trains to travel to Hampton, Virginia. Interestingly, I met a person aboard the train, and during the trip to Hampton, we developed what has become a lifelong friendship. His name was Edmund Brown and he was from New Haven, Connecticut. Once we arrived on the campus, we were assigned a room together as roommates. I decided that I would pursue a college degree in science and enrolled as pre-med. Edmund's college major was in business.

We were unaware at that time that there was a crisis that had developed because of all of the veterans returning who had served in World War II. Since we were freshmen, we suffered from the critical lack of housing facilities. We gained two other roommates, making a small room into a smaller one. Our new roommates were: Richard Smith from Richfield, North Carolina, and Dartridge Pennix from Farmville, Virginia. There were two bunk beds and a couple of desks to accommodate the four of us. Somehow, we survived our first year.

Nothing special or exciting happened at Hampton during my first year. I was busy trying to adapt from being in the military to acclimating to a civilian life. One thing that had an impact on me was the fact that Hampton was a very closed and close-knit society of faculty and students. The campus itself was completely isolated geographically from the city. Its closest neighbors were the Veterans' Cemetery, the Kecoughtan Hospital, and Fort Monroe Army Base. The campus is located on an island connected only by a few bridges.

During my second year, in 1948, I remained in the same building but moved to the first floor, where I had a larger room and fewer roommates. There was a little bit more excitement because the students, alumni members, and some faculty members protested against the president of Hampton Institute, Ralph Bridgman. I suspect that part of the disenchantment with him was caused by alumni members who felt that it was time to install a Negro as the president of Hampton Institute, a predominantly black college. Presently, I don't recall the issues that created the atmosphere for his removal, but it was taken under consideration by the board of directors, and he was removed from office. In short order, a president by the name of Alonzo Moron was selected. One of the biggest jokes that came about was from the main headline of one of the morning papers in Hampton, Virginia, which stated, and I quote: "*A. Moron* has just been installed as president of Hampton Institute."

Also during my second year, in 1948, I was faced with another decision and another challenge. The professor of Military Science and Tactics (PMST) at Hampton was Colonel Griner. He was a graduate of the United States Military Academy at West Point and a career soldier. He was responsible for recruiting students for the Reserve Officers' Training Corp (ROTC) program at Hampton. He was constantly examining scholastic records of male students who might qualify for officer training. So it was that I was called into consultation near the close of my sophomore year. He discussed many of the advantages that people who chose a military career have over their civilian counterparts.

It took a lot of effort on his part to get me to see and understand the advantages the military might give me. At that point, I had very little interest in rejoining any military establishment. My stubbornness resulted over the fact that I had been out of the military for approximately two and a half years. The fact that I was an ex-serviceman meant that I would be required to enroll in the third and fourth year of the ROTC program, which included a drill period and classes once a week.

The first carrot that he placed before me was to offer me a free physical exam at the military base of Fort Monroe. He stated that it would highlight my physical condition if I took the offer of the free exam, and it would give me a better picture of my physical condition since I had not had a physical in more than two and a half years. I came through this physical exam with flying colors. He then stated that if I were to enroll in the program, I would be sent to a summer camp in Massachusetts—with pay and a chance to see Cape Cod in the summer. In addition, I would receive a one-hundred-dollar per month stipend for the two years that I was enrolled in the course. I would receive this in addition to the school subsidy that I already received as a veteran. He assured me also that my status, as perceived by the girls, would be enhanced. This was true, because one of the major functions on the campus was the annual ROTC ball. Needless to say, I succumbed to the song of the turtle.

The year 1948 brought about other changes in my life and in my college activities. First, I received a "Dear John" letter from my girlfriend of four years, Opal Taylor. I was totally devastated by her rejection of me, and it had negative effects on my psychological emotions and spilled over into my college classwork and other activities. It took awhile to overcome these effects; most of them may have been eliminated when I acquired a new girlfriend.

The new girlfriend entered my life quite by happenstance, luck, and by coincidence. My future girlfriend—and later, wife—Geraldine Hooper (Geri) and I met during class registration in the fall of 1948. The registration took place in the gymnasium at Hampton Institute. I was seated on a row in front of her and one of my best friends, Buffington Falls. Mr. Falls, whom Geri knew from her hometown, was helping her with her registration. They were both from Northumberland County, Virginia. Falls was older than Geri and had been employed as the school bus driver when he was a high school student in the county. He enrolled at Hampton in 1946.

While they were going through the registration process, I overheard her ask him to ask me for a pencil. I turned around immediately and responded, "Freshman, I would prefer if you wanted to borrow my pencil, you ask me, not go through him."

I requested her name and her dormitory location and said that I would contact her later. Needless to say, this lead to an acquaintance, a love affair, and finally, a marriage that lasted fifty-one years. I had also developed some acquaintances with several other young women on the campus. Most notable was a young lady whose name was Iva Omega Jones. She was a freshman also, and she lived in the city of Hampton. There came a time when I had to make a choice between the two ladies. Based on my emotional feelings, I made the choice easily, and Iva lost!

For the next three years, Geri and I were a known couple as viewed by the college community of students. We went everywhere together: to all of the college functions, to the movies in the city, restaurants, and in churches in the city of Hampton and Newport News. Geri majored in English with a minor in education. Some of my close friends and card-playing buddies gave her the nickname of "Bill Jones Jr."

Often, my card-playing buddies and I gathered after classes, and sometimes during class times, if we were not in class, to hold card-playing sessions in the community building, Clark Hall. Sometimes, when she finished classes or was interested in going to the college grill or some other event taking place, she would come to my "haunt" and "beckon" to me to accompany her wherever she was desirous of going. It was during this time that one of the wiseacres would comment by saying, "Bill, there's Junior." Hearing her dulcet voice, I would immediately respond, and away I would go. Needless to say, this ended my career as a free man about town.

In 1948, I also got involved with a very popular campus organization. The traditional and historical clubs on the campus during this time were social clubs, not fraternities. There were five campus clubs. The men's clubs were the Olympic Social Club, Omicron, and Fidiamici. The women's clubs were the Phyllis Wheatley Club and Calliope. I affiliated with the Olympic Social Club. All of the rituals that one views in national fraternities and sororities were practiced by the clubs. They had programs to initiate new members. They wore sweaters with the club's emblems, and members recognized special greetings among themselves.

There was heavy competition between the groups. The major activity was the grand ball, which was held by each club following a basketball tournament between the men's clubs. Although they competed against each other, they recognized the need to communicate with each other on problems that needed to be addressed as a college community; therefore, they established an intercampus group called The Tri-Club Council. I learned a lot about how to operate a successful meeting, because the organization was structured and managed like a well-oiled corporation. It consisted of a president, vice president, secretary, treasurer, a sergeant at arms, and a number of committees. During my membership in the organization, I held two important positions: the sergeant at arms and the vice president. I believe that the position as sergeant at arms gave me the ability to understand the workings of a well-run organization. This was true because I had to learn from the "Bible" of organization operations, Robert's Rules of Order. So, if I learned nothing else from my involvement in the social club, that job gave me knowledge that I later applied in other organizational endeavors.

I was engaged in another group as a member of a Hampton class family, the college band. I came to Hampton with a background as a musician as a former member in a high school and college band at Albany State, Georgia. In addition, I had served as a bugler in the Navy Drum and Bugle Corps at Great Lakes Naval Station at Camp Moffitt in Illinois. Interestingly, when I first joined the Hampton Institute band, they wore ROTC uniforms. After I joined, we raised enough money, including a subsidy from the college, to buy our first true school civilian uniforms. They were navy blue with gold stripes and did not match the school colors. The band played for many of the school's functions, which included basketball games, football games, and parades in the cities on the peninsula. We also had concerts in Ogden Hall during certain periods. I really enjoyed being a band member because I met a large number of people who were majoring in different subjects. The band also performed at and was highly visible during the graduation ceremonies.

The colonel's predictions that he made in 1948 all came true. In the summer of 1949, after finishing my junior year at ROTC, which some of my closest friends had also joined, I went to summer camp at Camp Edwards, Massachusetts. There were twelve or thirteen colleges and universities represented at the camp, and all of the activities were always competitive between the schools. My school, Hampton Institute, was the only black college present at camp, and we always gave a good account of our presence. The PMST at that time was Colonel Moses, and he accompanied us to the camp that summer. The days were hot, but we endured all of the rigors of camp. We had classes and drills. We also had an opportunity to fire the big 90mm AA guns at pre-selected targets.

All of the schools' ROTC units at our camp were being trained as anti-aircraft and guided-missile units. So part of our exercise in the field involved practice firing 90mm AA guns at sleeves being towed by airplanes. Near the end of our stay at Camp Edwards, Hampton's group had a picnic near one of the bodies of water. We invited some of the local beauties to attend that affair. A military ball culminated the close of our activities there. After camp, I went back to Chicago to my summer job and subsequently back to Hampton for my senior year.

Beginning the first semester in January of 1950, my junior-class year, I settled into a familiar routine involving all of my campus activities. I attended my classes as a matter of course and pursued all of the extracurricular activities that I was obligated to join. For example, I practiced with the band and played for all of the engagements at which we were obligated to perform. I participated in all of the Olympic Social Club activities, and I went to all of the social functions, and needless to say, my sweetheart, Geri always accompanied me.

By this time, we had decided that we were comfortable in our relationship and were truly meant for each other. In the summer of 1950, she went to Washington, DC, to a job that she held at Ms. Kay's Toll House located in Silver Spring, Maryland. She had acquired the job as she followed the footsteps of her aunt, Lovey Porter, who had worked at the same restaurant many years before. That same summer, I attended the summer-school program at Hampton Institute. I took several science courses. The most interesting one was Inorganic Chemistry. Since I only had a couple of courses for the summer, most of the rest of the time was spent doing my usual card playing and enjoying the campus scenery and the beach-like atmosphere that was provided by the location of Hampton Institute on the James River.

Following the completion of my summer classes at school, I returned to Albany for the rest of the summer. During the time I was in Albany, I helped my parents design a new home that they planned to build on a lot on Central Street near Cordele Road on the east side of town. My senior year began in September of 1950, to be completed in June of 1951. My activities for that period included all of my aforementioned obligatory interests, both official and nonofficial.

For several years, we had gone through a period of seeing a serious problem not only at Hampton Institute, but also at many major colleges and universities. Many students were engaged in and caught stealing and buying course tests. This type of behavior was called "cribbing." Many of us were aware of how it was being done; quite often, students who worked in the various departments that served as assistants to professors were assigned the task of drafting up and completing the printing of tests. Once the final draft had been completed, these "trusted" students changed into chameleons. They displayed the more *seamy* side of their lives. That is, they copied and sold copies of exams to personal friends who were to take the course examination. When the professors became aware of the "cribbing" procedures, many of them changed tactics.

A particular professor that I recall at Hampton threw his class a real curveball! He was a math professor named Dr. Eshleman. When his test day arrived and he faced his class, most of them looked forward to him handing out the prepared test papers. He stated, "Your test is about to begin, and I am aware that many of the departments had been victimized by cribbers. Thus, I have your prepared test, and you may leave the classroom for a short period of time, and when you come back, I will have your prepared test ready."

When the class members returned from their break, Dr. Eshleman had copied all of his test questions onto the blackboard. He then reached in his pocket and pulled out a sheet of paper on which he had the materials that he had written on the board, and he stated, "You see, no one could steal Dr. Eshleman's test, because he had his test in his coat pocket."

The above-mentioned case was just one of the many cases of cribbing. I had a personal experience that took place in one of my classes, an organic-chemistry class under Dr. Fields. He was one of my most interesting professors. At that time, I'd had some conversations with him about his personal life. Because I was involved in the band and with music, I had become aware that Dr. Fields was an ex-musician who had played in Fletcher Henderson's world-renowned jazz band. Dr. Fields, as an undergraduate, matriculated at Fisk University—a very elite, traditional, black university located in Tennessee. Fletcher Henderson had been the band director at Fisk, and each summer, he took the band on tour to raise money for the university. After a period of time, he and the band members agreed to start a professional jazz group. So, he retired from the university and went on to become famous as one of the greatest jazz bands in the country. As I came to learn this about Dr. Fields, I inquired further about how he became a professor of chemistry. After leaving the band, he taught chemistry at Florida A&M University in Tallahassee, Florida. Later, he came to Hampton and started teaching organic chemistry.

I was in his class, and we took his final examination. Several of us, after seeing the exam, became aware that we had helped to tutor a few students on the day before the exam, and those students presented to us certain chemical problems that they needed help in solving. A couple of us saw the real exam, and we realized that several of these same problems appeared on the test. Interestingly enough, because organic chemistry is, for the most part, one of the most difficult subjects for most science students, by the time we came to the final test period, almost all of us were on the bubble. This situation, then, was ripe for the cribbers, and they took the opportunity to buy the test to pass the course. At the close of the test, as we walked out and headed back across the campus, three or four of us realized that someone had indeed seen and used a copy of Dr. Fields's test. After a short discussion, we decided that we would go back and apprise him of our suspicions. He took it under advisement and notified all of the students that there would be, on a certain date, a complete retake of his final exam. This time, there was no chance for cribbing, based on the way he conducted the exam.

A special and very interesting situation developed for me in 1950. A person from my past tried to reenter my life. One day, I got a telephone message to call a certain telephone operator in Hampton, Virginia. I called the number, and a voice came out of my past. It was my former girlfriend. She indicated that she was now married, and her husband was stationed temporarily at Fort Eustis, Virginia, and said she would like to meet with me to discuss a matter. I informed her that if she desired to have a meeting with me, it would need to be on the campus at Hampton. We then arranged a date and a time for me to meet her at one of the bus stops near the campus. We met and decided that we would go on campus to the campus grill.

We had a discussion for about a half hour. She told me that she was disenchanted with her husband and was planning to seek a divorce, and she wanted to know whether or not I was married. I was very straightforward about my social position at this particular time. I expressed the fact that I had been extremely devastated by her letter that she'd written to me dissolving our relationship, that it took me a number of months to overcome the devastation, and that, in the meantime, I had met and was in a very strong relationship with someone new. I leveled with her over the fact that what she had done in the past, I could never forgive or forget, and in addition, I could never trust her again. I explained that there were now three other people whose lives would be affected: her husband, her child, and my girlfriend, and I was not going to disrupt the lives of anyone else by changing my life. And so it went. She departed the campus, and I remained loyal and committed to my present girlfriend and later, wife, Geri.

At the end of my 1950 school year, I received my commission as a second lieutenant in the US Army Reserves, along with my best friend, Buffington E. Falls. Shortly after his commission, he entered active duty in the US Army. The next school year, I served as a member of the ROTC training staff.

My senior year ended, and I received my bachelor of science degree in biology. Playing for the graduating class of 1951 also marked the end of my membership in the Hampton Institute Marching Band.

After graduation, I went back to Albany, Georgia, to ponder my future steps. After a very short period of time, I realized that job opportunities were almost nil and none. And so it was that I remembered a statement that was made to me by the PMST at Hampton, Colonel Griner. He told me that if a situation such as the one I was faced with now ever came to bear on my life's goals, I had a few options. I could call on my military experience and accomplishments to help me over a rough spot in my life, or I could gamble on an unknown future. Thus, I decided to apply for a military tour of duty.

There were a number of reasons for my decision to reenter the service. First was the fact that this time, I would enter the service as an officer with the potential for a career guaranteed, and second, I could prepare to further my education by applying to a medical school to become a doctor. I knew that the medical career was probably not a feasible approach because neither my family nor I had the funds to support that endeavor. In addition, jobs were scarce, and the military appeared to be a knight in shining armor. I took out a request for active duty in late June and was taken aboard in August. This tour of duty was beneficial to both the military and me, because the United States was engaged in the Korean War, I needed a job, and they needed a warm body.

I reported for duty at Camp Stewart near Hinesville, Georgia, located approximately twenty miles from Savannah, Georgia, where most of our off-duty time was spent. I spent approximately six months in training there. I was assigned to the Forty-Fourth Anti-Aircraft Artillery (AAA) Gun Battalion, which consisted of four batteries and a headquarters battery. Each battery consisted of four 90mm guns and four quad-50 machine guns. Approximately 120 men were assigned to each battery as its complement. The conditions under which we existed on the post at Camp Stewart were second only to being on bivouac in the fields. Our quarters were crude, wooden buildings that were screened in and covered with canvas. There was a pot-bellied stove at each end of the building, and the building was lighted by several frosted light bulbs. There was a building, equally as crude in shape and function, with a shower-bath. We had a wooden mess-hall building. For entertainment, there was the Officer's Club, where we could play cards, drink beer, and entertain our guests.

My tour at Fort Stewart lasted from August of 1951 until February 1952. While at Camp Stewart, I initially served as the recruiting officer for my gun battalion. The army, in all of its infinite wisdom, had decided that in order to maintain an army of ready, willing, and able bodies, the term of duty for most of the active-duty personnel was to be extended. The easiest way to accomplish this was to set up recruiting efforts for soldiers on duty to extend their tours of duty. Some of these servicepeople had been away from home for long periods of time. The military offered them an amount of cash and a special, thirty-day furlough in exchange for an increase in their active duty time. As the recruiting officer, my job was to lecture to the enlisted personnel about the benefits to be received by those who volunteered to sign up for the extended tour of duty.

After about three months, I was reassigned to the battery and became the executive officer for Battery C, Forty-Fourth AAA Gun Battalion. This was under the leadership of the battery commander, Captain Iverson Mitchell, who was from Washington, DC. I accompanied him to all of the battalion commanders' meetings. After attending a number of these meetings, I became aware that there was no love lost between battery Commander Mitchell and the battalion commander, whose name I do not recall.

We trained with the troops and had them ready for site duty by January 1952. We were ordered to our duty site, which was in Camp Edwards, Massachusetts, in late January. By that time, the rift between the battalion commander and Captain Iverson had widened, and the battalion commander relieved him of the battery and installed me as the battery C commanding officer. This change meant that he would be transferred to another group, and I would be then charged with the responsibility of the rest of the training and our subsequent deployment to Camp Edwards.

Military Snubs

As Negro officers in a segregated service, we were often shown disrespect by both the white officers and noncommissioned ("noncoms"), as well as the ordinary enlisted GI. Consequently, we were on the lookout for snubs from all of the above mentioned. Since most of our time was spent on bases, we had many encounters and were not disappointed in our expectations.

On the post, I had one snub at one of the guard gateposts. When I drove up to the gate, the guard waved me through instead of saluting first. I went through, and after about a hundred feet, I stopped, backed up, chewed him out, made him salute, threatened to report him, and then moved on. All officers' automobiles had a special tab on the tag with an *O*, which identified them as military officers—so he had purposefully ignored me.

On another occasion, I went to the PX on the base to shop. At the entrance, a guard stands and is expected to salute all officers as they enter. As I entered, this guard just stood, motionless. Again, I promptly confronted him, chewed him out, forced him to salute, and threatened to report him.

In addition to when they were on official duty, any enlisted personnel meeting an officer on the street was expected to salute. Many of us noticed that some of the enlisted personnel, if they saw you and they were far enough away, would intentionally cross the street instead of coming forward to meet you head on to salute you. Quite often, if I recognized that as the intent, I, too, would cross so that they had to meet me head on.

After I had been located at Camp Stewart for about three months, I acquired "automobile-buying fever." So, I went into Hinesville to a used-car lot and purchased my first car, which was a 1950 Dodge Wayfarer convertible. It was maroon with a white top and leather seats. It was used, but it was beautiful to me. Seeing it on the lot, I knew that this was me. I could now feel that I had arrived. Many of my associates became my best friends because they could travel with me—and travel, we did.

Our in-town headquarters was a restaurant called the Shangri-La. It was a restaurant nightspot in the Harlem section of Savannah. It had great food and was a place to socialize and drink with friends. We became acquainted with some of the local beauties, and fun was had by all.

Savannah State College was near, so we attended football and basketball games and other social affairs. The army post at Camp Stewart was an interesting place to travel on because of the hazards that it provided. It was called Camp Swampy because of the area from which it was developed, which was swampland. So, we had birds, huge mosquitoes, snakes, deer, turtles, cattle, and even alligators.

The large animals had been fenced in accidentally when the camp was developed. At night, when one drove into camp, it was usually foggy, and striking cows lying on the road was a hazard that produced great fear. A large number of cars were damaged by the cows that were on the highway. Since some ditches along the roadside contained water, both water moccasins and alligators were a grave concern if one had to stop the car along the road for any reason in one of these areas. I did not develop any serious relationships in or near Savannah, because my main squeeze was finishing off her senior year at Hampton.

My first long trip in this buggy was taken when I returned to Hampton for its homecoming in October 1951. A friend of mine, a fellow officer who was also from Hampton Institute by the name of Austin Monsanto, accompanied me on the trip to Hampton. He was training in automotive mechanics. So I was confident that we could embark from Hinesville and arrive in Hampton before the homecoming. When we started, I had the shock of my life, because after I had driven for a period of time with him acting as the navigator, I discovered that we had traveled for a fairly long distance going the wrong direction. We went south toward Florida instead of north going to Hampton, Virginia. I soon corrected the course and started the long drive toward Hampton. We arrived in Hampton just a short time before kickoff. The trip was not without some added excitement along the way.

After I had driven for a long time, I was jaded and a little tired. I decided to put him under the wheel for a few hours of driving. Fortunately, before I took a nap, I observed his driving habits and ability, and I decided that removing him as soon as possible was in our best interest. Almost every time, when a car approached him, he would slow down to a crawl. The crowning blow took place when we crossed a river bridge, and I thought I smelled paint burning, indicating that he was scraping the bridge. It was that close! I took him out from under the wheel and proceeded to drive until later, when I pulled over to the nearest gas station and slept for a while. After a few hours, we continued our trip to the campus at Hampton, and we made it just in time before the kick-off of the football game. We spent the rest of the day and evening socializing, and after a good night's sleep, we proceeded back to my military base at Camp Stewart.

In December, I contacted Geri to see if she could get permission from her grandmother, Martha Basey, to allow her to accompany me to my parents' home in Albany, Georgia. Permission was granted, and I made arrangements to have Geri meet me in Savannah, Georgia, and we would journey to Albany. When she arrived in Savannah, I picked her up, and we drove from Savannah to Albany, arriving there the next morning. I introduced her to all of my family members present, and my mother arranged for her to be housed with us throughout the Christmas holiday. My mother accepted her with open arms as though she were a long lost daughter. Subsequent to our marriage later, the relationship between my mother and Geri grew and lasted until my mother's death in 1998—forty-seven years later. For my girlfriend and my mother, this was love at first sight.

My mother was overjoyed when I informed her that I planned to marry Geri. To assist in these plans, my mother accompanied me to a jewelry store, where we purchased the engagement and wedding rings. My mother was able to keep the secret until I proposed marriage to Geri on Christmas morning, December 25, 1951. Needless to say, she must have had some inkling of my intentions, but she never showed any emotions prior to the moment of the truth. She was very gracious and appeared to be very happy to have our relationship advanced to the ultimate level expected in a man-and-woman relationship. I promised her that I would make an attempt to complete the loop by writing a letter to Grandma Basey, who had reared her, asking for her permission and blessings in our engagement. At that time, we did not set a specific date, but it was generally understood that the date would come only after her graduation from college.

Part of the uncertainty was primarily based on the fact that I did not know what orders from the military might interfere with our timing. After the Christmas holiday, she went back to Hampton University, and I went back to Camp Stewart with the greatest mission of my life already accomplished.

In February 1952, my battalion was ordered to Camp Edwards in Massachusetts to prepare for our site duty in the area of Fort Devens, Massachusetts. We traveled in convoy from Camp Stewart, Georgia, to Camp Edwards, Massachusetts, through the following states: South Carolina, North Carolina, Virginia, Pennsylvania, New York,

Connecticut, and finally Massachusetts. We stopped at and stayed overnight at several camps or forts between Georgia and Massachusetts. One of these overnight stops was at Fort Eustis, Virginia. This was fortunate for a couple of other officers in my battalion and me because Eustis is located near Hampton, Virginia. So, several of us embarked to a trip to Hampton's campus to see our girlfriends. Even though it was past the socializing hour at the dorms, the matrons allowed us a short visit with our ladies. We were all aware that if we had not been in uniform, they would not have been so gracious.

Shortly after the visit, we went back to Eustis, from where we departed the next morning. The convoy proceeded all the way to Massachusetts with only one minor accident, which was caused by a civilian driver who ignored warnings that a convoy of military vehicles was passing through, and he should not have broken into the line of vehicles. In breaking into the file of vehicles, he accidentally struck a truck and damaged his auto. There was no personal injury or any serious damage to any vehicle. When we informed him that it was his mistake and that there was no injury to any person and no damage of serious consequence to the military vehicle, he moved on.

We checked in as a unit onto the base at Camp Edwards. We remained there long enough to prepare the unit for its role in the defense of the northeastern corridor of the United States. From February to April 1952, the Forty-Fourth AAA Gun Battalion stayed at Camp Edwards. In April 1952, I was ordered to attend a four-month course called the Associate Basic Officer's Course for AAA officers to be held at Fort Bliss, Texas.

When I retired from the military, I moved into the Sydnor residence, and we remained there for a few months. We could not find a decent, reasonably priced apartment, so we moved across the river, into southeast DC to the Parkland complex, which was built by Morris Cafritz and managed by Henry Davis, a Hampton alumnus. This was a very unique facility where we lived for eleven years. All of our children but one, Gerald, were born there.

One of the most challenging periods of our marriage was quite possibly from the second year, 1954, through the year 1987. We had to decide, without receiving any training, how we were going to deal with problems related to rearing children. It happened so fast that we were subjected to on-the-job training. We began by recognizing what our goals in life would be. We decided, from the outset, that we both needed our jobs in order to secure a comfortable standard of living—for example, living in a safe and comfortable area for raising children, an area containing good schools that featured middle-class surroundings.

It began after the first child, Valerie, was born and continued through the birth of the three others, who were born approximately twenty months apart. We both were on a 9:00 a.m. to 5:00 p.m. work schedule, so we needed childcare. At first, we paid for in-home childcare. We made it through that way for thirteen years and then we were able to buy our first home. We purchased it in August of 1964 in Hillcrest, one of the most prestigious areas in DC. It was an all-white suburban community located on the borderline of Prince George's County, Maryland, and southeast Washington, DC. At that time, the population was approximately fifteen- to eighteen thousand; today, it is approximately twenty thousand.

Valerie was approximately ten years old when we moved to Hillcrest. She was enrolled in a private school called Kiddie's College that took kids in after diaper training and went from first to sixth grade. Melba and Billy were three and a half and one and a half years old, and they both received in-home care. Our last child, Gerald, was born approximately one month after we moved to Hillcrest. My mother came up from Georgia to help Geri while she took leave from work.

We were able to afford a maid-service lady who served in-house care, and she prepared meals and did other housework, such as washing clothes. The maid was usually on the job from 9:00 a.m. to 5:00 p.m. However, some of the caretakers didn't have transportation, so we'd pick them up in the morning and carry them home in the evening. We had to be ready for emergencies, so we never felt comfortable until the weekends or holidays. We finally were able to locate a facility that served all of our needs and provided professional care so that we felt comfortable while we were working.

When the children reached school age, we had a good caretaker to be at the house to care for the kids until we came home. At this time, they were going to Anne Beers Elementary School in the neighborhood. It was located about four or five blocks from our house. Melba, Billy, and Gerald were able to walk to school. They continued at Anne Beers from first through the sixth grade and completed their elementary years there. The three then entered junior high at John Phillip Sousa High. It was an outstanding school with a great reputation for producing scholastic achievers. It was named after John Phillip Sousa, the former marine music director, composer, and arranger for music specifically used in military parades. He was also well known for designing the instrument known as the Sousaphone.

At that time, junior high was for grades six, seven, and eight, and senior high was ninth, tenth, eleventh, and twelfth grades. Melba finished three years at Sousa, and her high school was McKinley Tech High School. Billy also finished three years at Sousa and then entered Woodson High School. The reason Gerald spent only two years at Sousa was because Billy had learned to drive and didn't want to go to McNamara Catholic School. So, we allowed Billy to enter Woodson, and as a chore, he had to drive Gerald to McNamara and continue from there to Woodson. Gerald transferred from Sousa to Bishop McNamara and matriculated there for five years.

CHAPTER VIII

Hillcrest Subdivision: My Home Area

My reason for including information about the Hillcrest subdivision is to continue to highlight the racial situation in the District of Columbia, which mirrored what was taking place nationwide. It primarily gives everyone a look into the segregated-housing dilemma that existed at that time in the United States.

We moved into Hillcrest in 1964, approximately four years prior to the federal housing amendment. When we moved there, there were only three or four African-American families in Hillcrest. The subdivision was approximately 99 percent white, while today it is 97 percent African-American and 3 percent other ethnicities. In 1964, there were only a few small businesses in the Fairfax Village area and at the intersection of Alabama Avenue and Naylor Road. What was missing in both areas was an upscale restaurant, although there was one Sears store and a movie theater.

Most of the African-Americans moving in the area were middle-income, white-collar workers with children whose career aspirations were very high. They were expected to go to college and to continue to graduate schools and beyond. A couple of years after we moved in, around

1966–1968, Mayor Marion Barry lived in the subdivision, and along with him came many of his department managers. The present mayor, Muriel Bowser, and a few of her staff now live in the neighborhood.

When my fiancée, Geri, was completing her college studies in 1952, and preparing to obtain her degree from Hampton, we agreed to set the date for our wedding. The wedding had to be carried out on the military base at Fort Bliss, Texas, on June 14, 1952, with the consent and the blessing of her grandmother. Following her graduation, Geri had received an offer to teach in the elementary department of schools for Negroes in Arlington, Virginia. During her trip to Arlington for the confirmation of her appointment and for the orientation of new school employees, she met several very important people. Two new acquaintances were Mr. and Mrs. Sydnor, a couple who lived in Arlington and originally came from her neck of the woods in Northumberland County.

Geri was assigned to work in a neighborhood called Green Valley at Kemper (later Kemper-Drew) Elementary School. It was here that she witnessed a great moment when Kemper School was rededicated and the name of Charles Drew was annexed to it. Dr. Charles Drew will forever be associated with the study of blood—primarily because he pioneered the establishment of blood banks that were created to save lives, especially in the military during the Second World War.

Fortunately, for transportation purposes, Mrs. Sydnor, who could drive, also worked as an elementary teacher at Kemper. Because of her background in education, which she received at Hampton Institute under the tutelage of Dr. Mitchell, Geri was considered to be an outstanding prospect by the Arlington school-system managers. She worked in that school system for ten years.

During her first few months at Kemper, we rented a room in the home of the Sydnors. However, we decided early on that we needed an apartment by ourselves. We tried unsuccessfully to locate an apartment in Arlington, Virginia. In the meantime, we became aware that a huge apartment complex was being developed in southeast Washington, DC, by the Cafritz family. The manager of the complex was an alumnus of

Hampton, named Henry Davis , so that made our quest for an apartment a foregone conclusion. The complex was located near a troubled area of southeast DC, but this housing project proved to be a rose located in the midst of a thorny area.

It was a great experience to be in that community because the management screened all applicants and leased only to young upwardly mobile individuals. So, approximately 75–80 percent of the applicants were high school and college graduates. All were upwardly mobile African-Americans with good jobs, such as teachers, government workers, lawyers, doctors, ministers, policemen, firemen, and so forth. The manager, Henry Davis, allowed some community people to set up a hobby shop in the basement in one of the buildings. It included one area for TV and radio repairs, an upholstery shop, and a cabinet-making shop. I worked with a friend, Avery Horton, a chemist from Hampton who managed the cabinet shop. We built bars and bookcases, finished basements, made coffee tables, and so forth. I learned a lot about cabinetry, including furniture refinishing and so forth, that I utilized later after buying a home.

We lived in that complex for more than ten years. Because the manager was a Hamptonian, a huge number of Hampton alumni were housed in the development.

Through other connections in the school system, she met a couple from Waco, Texas. The schools in Arlington were at the beginning of their summer break, so this newfound couple from Waco was headed home. They planned to travel by car from Arlington, Virginia, to Waco, Texas. This trip was a very fortunate circumstance in that Geri was invited to travel with them all the way to Waco, and she fortunately discovered that she could take a train from Waco directly into El Paso, Texas.

When she arrived at El Paso, I had made all of the arrangements for the wedding to take place at one of the churches on the post at Fort Bliss. I had also arranged a place for us to receive room and board following the wedding. I had met a couple that owned a very nice house within a ten-minute commute to Fort Bliss. The wedding was attended by several of my friends and her friends from Hampton who were also stationed at Fort Bliss. I had also met another couple from New Jersey, the Osbornes, who were stationed there and were a young, newly wed couple. He served as my best man, and she served as the matron of honor. The ceremony was conducted by an army chaplain and a colonel, whose name was Thornton. Following the wedding ceremony, we all went to the fort officer's club for the celebration. Since I was there in class, we could not go off to any special place for the honeymoon. So, we continued the daily routines until the classes ended in August of 1952.

When my military classwork at Fort Bliss was completed, I had orders to report back to Camp Edwards, my aforementioned duty station. Because I had at least a week for furlough, we decided to travel, by car, north to Chicago and, finally, east to Massachusetts. The Chicago part of our trip was planned so that my new bride could meet some of the members of my family, primarily my sister and her family and Uncle Willie, as well as his wife, Laura. Despite the lousy accommodations we experienced on the trip (which was common because of our race), we proceeded to travel all the way to Chicago with one overnight stay in Saint Louis, Missouri.

We arrived in Chicago on a Saturday with plans to leave the following Monday. However, the first night of our stay in Chicago was a very emotionally devastating period. My sister was living in a low-income, poverty-stricken area, which was an area where numerous crimes were committed. I should have known better than to stop over in such an area. Initially, I was not overly concerned, because during several summers in the late forties, I had lived in that community.

Now, I'm sure that the thugs noticed a car with out-of-state tags and decided that this was "manna from heaven." So overnight, the trunk of my car was broken into and all items of any value were stolen; the remaining items were scattered on the ground around the car. My sister was awakened the next morning by neighbors who saw the vandalized car and were aware that it belonged to one of my sister's relatives—me. For us, it ruined our trip, and we could not wait for Monday morning to come so we could leave that hellhole. The greatest loss was my wife's wedding regalia. I knew we could replace all of her other clothing that was stolen. On the other hand, I had no losses, because they did not need any military uniforms.

Arriving in Massachusetts, for the rest of the furlough, we went directly to live with friends who were Hampton graduates, like we were. Henry and Doris Sitgraves were military friends of mine who were also stationed in the Camp Edwards area and were living in Cape Cod. Doris informed my new wife that we could stay there, but she would have to cook for her new husband, as this would provide her with great experience in the area of taking care of him. The fun began on that first day with the first meal that Geri attempted to prepare. It was then that I was aware that cooking was not her forte.

She attempted to cook pancakes; however, no one had given her any training in that culinary art process. So, her first move was to whip up a batch of flour, milk, and eggs in a bowl, and she poured the total content into a skillet. Needless to say, as it began to rise and bubble, it spilled over onto the stove area and created a grand mess. Doris arrived in the kitchen, pronto, and explained to her that maybe for the rest of her marriage, she should hire a housekeeper, unless she was interested in creating an early demise for her new husband. In other words, her cooking was going to kill him! In early September of 1952, Geri returned to her school assignment in Arlington, Virginia.

After finishing the AAA Basic Officer's Course at Fort Bliss, I returned to Camp Edwards. My battery was attached to the 704th AAA Gun Battalion under the Forty-Fifth Brigade at Fort Devens, Massachusetts. Our anti-aircraft defense position was located on Deer Island. It was best known as a minimum-security prison facility. The prisoners that were housed there were described as drunks and homeless people who would intentionally become incarcerated so that they were able to escape the harsh winters found in the northeastern Massachusetts area. In addition to my battery, there were two other attachments located at this compound. There was an all-white AAA gun battery equivalent to mine, and a naval detachment was also located there. The other AAA battery and my battery both operated under the Forty-Fifth Brigade.

Since my battery was almost an all-Negro outfit, except for two second lieutenants and one warrant officer, who were Caucasian, we were not well received by the other groups. The navy detachment probably was the most agitated, because they were provided military housing on the compound. Therefore, as expected, their worries were the general stereotype attitudes feared by most Caucasians that Negroes were uncivilized and were to be shunned at all costs. Because all of us were assigned by the military departments, they had no options but to coexist with us.

We were always on an alert status because we were part of the North American defense command utilized to protect against enemy air strikes. It meant that during alerts, my troops had to cross a lot of the hallowed grounds occupied by the Caucasians.

The white AAA unit had been on station there for a while before we arrived and did not want to share any of the facilities. For an example, there was a recreational building where the troops could relax and engage in activities such as basketball and other types of physical exercise. On one occasion, my men used the recreational facility while the whole white battery was away for approximately a week. When they returned, the battery commander confronted me, complaining that my men had left the recreation center in shambles and that they would be barred entirely from the use of the facility if that happened again.

The very next complaint that I received was his concern about my men visiting his PX (post exchange). This time, he came to my office and tried to use his first-lieutenant rank to dress me down and intimidate me in my office in front of my staff. This was his mistake number two and/or three. I informed him that his conduct and his attitude would not be tolerated and that if his tirade continued, I would have my personnel in the orderly room physically eject him and his executive officer. I further admonished him that when any superior-rank officer entered my office, his rank would be left hanging on the outside of my door when he entered my orderly room. He got the message and calmed down, and then we talked civilly. There were no more problems afterward.

The strangest thing happened that addressed irony. A few weeks after our confrontation, an order that all of the AAA batteries in the area were to be desegregated was received from the Forty-Fifth Brigade Headquarters. All battery commanders were ordered to meet at headquarters and briefed on the moves to desegregate. We all met in a large room and were seated at a table with a personnel roster of the batteries. However, at this exercise, only two batteries were to be broken down and regrouped: the two that were located on Deer Island. So, ironically, my antagonist and I were required to exchange personnel who had earlier had a problem with coexisting. The breakdown left each battery approximately a fifty-fifty complement of Negroes and Caucasians. As I recall, no officer personnel were involved in the exchange. The whole process was carried without any incidences, and peace and harmony prevailed.

During my stay on Deer Island, most of the entertainment the troops received was in some of the clubs in Boston. I recall a couple of trips I took to the city, when I was entertained by Dizzie Gillespie and Red Fox.

In January 1953, my battery was ordered to proceed to Niagara Falls, New York. We were directed to set up an AAA defense of the hydroelectric power plants in and around Niagara Falls. My tour of duty lasted only for a few weeks.

During the end of my tour of duty, my wife was off for her holiday break. So, we got an opportunity to enjoy Niagara Falls in the winter. I next notified my battery commander about my intent not to further extend my tour of active duty. In order to try to persuade me from leaving, he promised to recommend me for an immediate promotion to first lieutenant. When I refused his offer, he congratulated me on my outstanding performance under his command and offered his prayers for my continued success. No matter what road I chose to follow, I was off to see the Wizard of Oz.

CHAPTER IX

My Career in Government

MY NEXT MOVE WAS a journey over an unknown and unchartered road. Coming out of the military, I had no job, nor any prospects. Once upon a time, I had aspired to go to medical school, but since I did not have the money to take such a venture, and as a newlywed, I wanted to start a family and to create a better life. The year was 1953, and "equal rights and opportunities" were still only a dream for Negroes. Negroes were undergoing the nightmares that had haunted them since President Rutherford B. Hayes sold them out after his election. After paying a political debt, he removed the forces that had maintained the peace (the Union Army). The Ku Klux Klan and other vigilante groups replaced the Union Army, and the laws of miscegenation and laws supporting the right to vote public accommodation and other segregation and discrimination edicts sealed the Negroes' fate. So, I came to the Washington, DC, area to face an uncertain future.

I arrived in the DC area in January 1953. With no job prospects and no understanding as to how the job market in this area worked, I was at a total loss. I soon learned that my first approach would be to go to the U.S. Employment Services Office to see what jobs were available. The questionnaire that I filled out had a few positive questions that I answered that were very helpful. The main question was asking about my college major. So, it alerted the agency to be on the lookout for entry-level jobs that a college graduate should apply for. After I went to the agency, they gave me a call and an offer to take a six-month temporary job with Immigration Services. At that time, a large number of college grads worked as janitors, taxi drivers, waiters, policemen, and firemen and in places such as the postal department. Most Negroes in the government jobs worked in the basements carrying out these menial jobs. My job at the Immigration Agency consisted of sorting cards relating to making certain that immigrants were following immigration laws.

At the beginning of 1953, after my tour of duty, I worked in this immigration office for about six weeks, and I quit after I received a notice from the US Employment Service that they had a job available for me in the science area. This job was also a temporary job that offered three months of employment. I was offered a job as a GS-4 medical biology technician working at the Food and Drug Administration laboratory. This medical biology technician job was in an animal laboratory at a salary of approximately $2,700 a year. I always equated my salary with the cost of a new Dodge Coronet that I had purchased approximately six months prior to leaving the military, which cost approximately $2,500.

I received the job as a temporary replacement for a young, white woman who left the FDA on maternity leave for approximately three months. This allowed me some time to ponder and study my situation. What I found out was that the government did not use the same yardstick for qualifying people of science as was used in the industry. For example, they examined your resume in the sciences for becoming a professional biologist or a chemist and found those qualified who had a BA or BS in those fields. To get promoted from grade to grade, one had to take certain classes to be promoted to the next-highest level. Technicians had a very difficult time qualifying for professional classifications without a degree. The technical promotional scales advanced one grade level at a time as follows: GS-2, GS-3, GS-4, GS-5, and GS-6, while a professional biology rating started at GS-5 to GS-7, GS-9, and GS-11, and then to GS-12, GS-13, and so forth until reaching the highest level, which was a GS-16.

I worked for three months, as per the order of employment, and then received an additional thirty days because the young lady decided to ask for an extension of one month. I would've been unemployed completely after the lady technician returned, except faith intervened. Ironically, when she returned, there was a mass firing of animal handlers that took place in one of the labs, triggered by the misconduct of these animal handlers. I took a downgrade to animal handler in order to survive. I was required to feed and water animals and to do a myriad of custodial services, such as cleaning animal cages, and any other odd jobs as required.

There were several white PhD professionals that were aware of my college qualifications, and they were trying to assist me in moving upward. One of these persons approached me about working in his lab for him. In addition to having me do some animal work in his lab, he also taught me some of the technical skills that I could use on my resume to qualify for a better job. Later, a GS-6 technician was promoted into another lab, and I got his previous position. But at the level of a GS-3, I was a medical bio-technician. I worked at that level for a couple of years before being promoted as a GS-4. In the meantime, I checked on a civil-service announcement, and I qualified and certified for a position as a GS-5 biologist; however, no position existed at the FDA so that I could obtain that rating.

Lady Luck smiled on me in the name of Dr. Ann Burke, who was the person who hired me for the temporary position at the FDA. She was the sister-in-law of the television star Arthur Godfrey, who reigned supreme during the 1950s and 1960s. She was able to get me a transfer to the National Institute of Health. She found out that one of her friends and fellow associates had a laboratory position for a GS-5 biologist. Because I was already certified, I was able to transfer from the FDA to the National Institute of Health (NIH) in that role. I was now on a track as a professional scientist.

The period of my new employment at NIH lasted only a couple of months. There was another Negro male in my section who was a GS-7 and was not in good standing with his boss. The boss wanted to fire him and wanted me to "rat" on him for abusing weekend overtime, but I refused to cooperate. Seeing this move to oust a fellow employee who was black, I knew I might be next!

A few days later, I called my division administrative officer at the FDA, whom I knew well, about returning to the FDA. He was very pleased to hear that and offered to take me back at my old job, but with the new rating. Therefore, I was the first professional Negro hired by the FDA labs as a research scientist. My career took off slowly, but on a steady climb. Part of the reason for the slow climb was that I did not have an advanced degree in biology. Part of my ability to move forward was accomplished due to my early experience in working hard, learning fast, being diligent in my work ethic, listening, studying, and understanding personalities as well as having a good personality myself. I also learned that one always needs a good sponsor, usually your supervisor, to pave the way by encouraging you to produce and learn more.

I was blessed to have such a person to help me in all areas. I had been in my agency for approximately seven or eight years when she was hired by the FDA. Her name was Jean Taylor, and she had a PhD in pharmacology/toxicology from Rochester University in New York. She had done her thesis studying the fluoridation of drinking water. It was a study that helped to foster the use of fluorides instead of chlorides for water purification. She was one of the rare university graduates whose major and PhD was in the field of toxicology.

Everything I learned and know about toxicology, I received through her very able and capable mentoring. She guided me throughout the last twenty-plus years of my career. She took a hands-on approach in teaching me to prepare abstracts and papers of my work for submission and acceptance by scientific boards and articles to be published in a variety of journals. I learned how to develop protocols for scientific studies and protocols for good laboratory-animal practices. I learned from her how to present my research before my peers, who often were our greatest critics. She was very meticulous about the method of writing. She suggested that I write my thoughts on paper, regardless of the order, and consider that as my first draft. Second, I should organize the paper chronologically according to subject matter. This meant that the most important approach was to get started and edit the paper later. In addition, she encouraged me to take scientific courses at area universities that would pave the way not only for academic achievement, but also for job promotion.

Looking back over my career, I have required a certain degree of realism on how to develop a successful career. In addition to acquiring the necessary formal education and training, one must cultivate a relationship with someone whom I will call a mentor and/or a sponsor. These two persons may be one and the same. The mentor teaches and nurtures the pupil, and the sponsor finds and smoothes the way for the pupil to advance in his chosen endeavor. My mentor, sponsor, and yea, my guardian angel, was Dr. J. M. Taylor, whom I worked for, and with, for more two decades. Her approval was always in the form of suggestions about formal courses to pursue at the local colleges and universities as well as classes and training offered in federally sponsored programs. This type of approach was best suited for me based on me having to be the family man and working on my career and other goals.

Without discussing any plans relative to our future together, Geri and I went forward preparing for whatever was ahead. One thing that we never discussed a plan for was having children. She complained of some female problems that might interfere with her being able to have children. So we made an appointment to see a female specialist. Our choice of physicians was an unfortunate one, in that he showed a lack of fundamental matters dealing with patients. After he performed the initial exam on my wife, he failed to include me, her husband, in a conference to explain his discoveries of her condition. She told me later that she was not impressed with how he performed the exam. He was a physician of our race whom we were trying to patronize. We located another person whose professional mannerisms were almost perfect.

One of the reasons I have lofty expectations for people in the medical profession is due to my working in navy hospitals and medical dispensaries for more than two and a half years during World War II. One of my requirements was to see a consortium of doctors who teamed up working as specialists with one or more available to serve patient emergencies. I also wanted the doctor to be a staff member of a quality hospital. My wife and I located such a team and were very pleased with our first visit to doctors Lady and Leonard. Dr. Lady examined Geri, and after the exam, he called her and me into his office. He placed a model of the internal female organs on his desk and outlined the problem area. He then gave his recommendation for treatment. His diagnosis was that the uterus was out of alignment, which was created by weakened muscles in the womb area. He recommended a special exercise for Geri to perform, and several months later, we had evidence that the condition had been corrected.

Dr. Lady's diagnosis and treatment proved to be correct, because on October 1, 1954, our first precious bundle of joy, Valerie Lynette Jones, was born. It was an exciting time for us, and we were blessed by the arrival of my mother from Georgia, who helped us with the baby for more than six weeks. My mother was overjoyed because Valerie was the first grandchild born to of her sons.

Valerie provided the two of us with many hours of joy, because there was no other sibling for more than six-plus years. She was a very smart baby who was also beautiful. We took a number of trips with her, including one to Houston, Texas, which was the most memorable. I was a military reservist and had to take a tour of duty to Fort Bliss in Texas. In the summer of 1956, we took the trip by car from Washington to Houston, where Geri and Valerie spent two weeks with our friends in Houston while I traveled on to Fort Bliss.

The trip was not without the usual problems expected and experienced by Negroes traveling by car. Public accommodations were segregated throughout the South, so we knew that the only places that we could expect to have good hotel accommodations and good restaurants was in large, Southern cities like Birmingham, Alabama. So, for most of the trip, we expected to travel and not stop until we had made it more than four hundred miles.

Our best rest stop came in Birmingham, Alabama, at the A. G. Gaston Motel. Mr. Gaston was a Negro entrepreneur who owned several enterprises such as funeral homes, motels, insurance companies, and other properties. His motel was very modern and was as beautiful as any white motel. They also provided their guest with souvenirs as they departed.

Our trip was marred by only one incident that took place in Poplarville, Mississippi. Before leaving Birmingham, we went to a grocery store and stocked up on enough food to have sandwiches and drinks to last us all the way to Houston. We drove into Mississippi and stopped in a public park to eat our noon meal. We observed some redneck workers, but they kept their distance. I started on the road again and then decided to gas up and make a bathroom stop. As I drove into the station and saw the usual restroom signs, "White Men," "White Women," and "Coloreds," I made a U-turn around the pumps and got back on the highway.

I had gone about a half mile when I was pulled over by the local redneck constable. He accused me of reckless driving because he had observed me pulling out of the gas station, kicking up gravel as I entered the highway. He ordered me to follow him to a trailer where the justice of the peace was located. He took me in and stated his case. I was asked to plead guilty or not. I said, "Not Guilty," and the justice of the peace said that would cost me $13.95 ($12.95 for the charge and one dollar for the witness who rode in the car with the constable). This was the true Mississippi justice. We left, and as soon as we got on the road, I chuckled because I would've been in serious trouble had he noticed my .25 automatic pistol on my car seat. I am sure my style of travel didn't help, because I had a brand-new Dodge Custom Royal Lancer. It was pink, black, and white. We experienced no other irritation on our trip to Texas and back to Washington.

***

As two working parents with a young baby, we had to pay babysitters for services. So, we had approximately three years of headaches finding reliable people, which meant that most of the time, in the fall and winter, we carried the baby out for daycare. We were extremely happy when she got old enough to go to school. We enrolled Valerie in a private school called Kiddie's Kollege, where she stayed for several years. The DC school board set up a special experimental elementary school called Amidon. The experimental program continued into junior high at Jefferson Junior High School. When Valerie finished Jefferson, we enrolled her in a girls' catholic school called Notre Dame Academy.

During the school year, we had a hectic schedule of getting breakfast and preparing Valerie for the babysitter and later for school. Geri worked in Virginia from 1952 to 1962, and she never learned to drive. So, I was the designated chauffer for her and some of her compatriots who also taught in South Arlington. Fortunately for me, I worked in southwest DC, across the river from Virginia. So, I had to return to my job after dropping them off at school, and I survived that for approximately ten years.

We were very innovative in the way that we utilized our transportation. I was the chauffer for Geri's group and also for taking Valerie to and from school. She was in school, which was located just a few blocks from where I worked. After school, she went to the nearby public library, which was right near my job. Because of all these challenges, our lives were well organized to meet all of our needs. The beauty of the situation with Valerie was that I was always within a half of a mile of her from elementary through high school. She was a model student, so we had no disciplinary problems. She had great study habits and was eager to achieve.

A few years after Valerie was born, Geri was pregnant, and it lasted only a couple months before the fetus was aborted, where she ultimately had a miscarriage. We were both very disappointed; however, we were happy that she went through the trauma of losing the baby without causing her to experience any mental or physical damage.

On May 16, 1961, we were again blessed with the birth of another bouncing baby, Melba Lynn Jones. She, too, was a healthy, beautiful baby girl. Once again, my mother came to Washington and stayed for approximately three months and provided her special, undivided attention to Geri and the two girls.

The die had been cast for rearing our children, and we learned a lot, often through experience, the hard way. With Melba, we still had the neighbors who helped as babysitters until she reached school age. With at least one of the babysitters, we had an in-house caretaker. She cleaned, washed clothing, and did a few minor chores; however, her main job was babysitting Melba. When Melba reached three or four years in age, we enrolled her in Kiddie's Kollege, as we had done with Valerie. Melba's first school enrollment was in first grade at Anne Beers, a neighborhood elementary school. When she reached junior high, she enrolled at John Phillip Souza in southeast DC. Later, she enrolled at McKinley Tech High School. Melba was a good student throughout all of the school levels, but she showed very little, or no interest in extracurricular activities at all.

She was, from childhood, a very easygoing, happy person with a good personality. Melba's program had been predetermined because she was the second girl born approximately six and a half years after Valerie. She didn't spend much time as the baby because William "Billy" Jones, the first boy, was born on January 1, 1963, approximately twenty months after Melba's birth. And, our next son, Gerald Alan Jones, was born on September 20, 1964, twenty months after Billy. Our final three children were so close in age that they required special babysitters who could handle three kids. Geri was teaching in DC shortly after Melba was born, and she knew a number of people who provided tips to us to help us find reliable babysitters.

One of the most notable was Johnny Mae Johnson. She had a childcare center, and we used her services for the last three children. She helped with all of our needs, which included any and every emergency. Our relationship started with her daycare service, and it included her first husband, Mr. Thomas, who worked with me at the FDA. Her husband worked part-time as a cab driver. His career as a scientist and cabbie ended tragically one Saturday as he was driving one of his customers. The customer held him up and then shot and killed him and took away his wedding ring. The murderer made his way to California and later made a grave mistake. He went to a bar and was bragging to a person that he met in Los Angeles about what he had done in Washington, DC. The bar patron reported the incident to the police, and the murderer was apprehended. The irony of it all was that he was wearing Thomas's diamond ring. He was later extradited back to Washington, where the court found him guilty of murder, and he went to prison.

Johnny Mae, a very strong woman, bounced back from that ordeal and continued to provide her community with valuable service in childcare. She was one of the most congenial, sensitive, cooperative persons that I ever met.

The aforementioned decades were critical times in the life of my family and me. Rearing children and meeting their needs meant that we were fulfilling commitments that we felt were necessary. So, Geri and I decided that we would not carry the load without sacrificing our own continuing-education plans. Dr. Taylor was aware of my personal goals as my career was developing, as well as my family concerns and accomplishments. She kept abreast of my community involvement and my volunteer work in the Department of Health, Education and Welfare (HEW), which is now called the Department of Health and Human Services. She knew that I was working tirelessly with civil-rights issues, primarily serving as an EEO counselor from 1967–1982.

I was engaged twice per week in teaching math to technicians working on their GEDs. I taught lab technology to a few ex-prisoners who were trying to start new lives. She allowed me to take time off to perform many volunteer assignments. I worked as a volunteer on my local community school board, as well as being the president of a parent-teacher club, and I was active in the neighborhood civic association. Jean always took my activities seriously, and she entered me to win some of the awards sponsored by the Department of HEW. One such award that I won was the first EEO award given by that department in 1974. She always encouraged me to take special, work-related courses and attend special meetings, seminars, and technical courses that got me prepared for much of the research in which our unit was engaged. There came a time when I was tapped by the administrators for certain management and supervisory courses that lead me to be promoted to a supervisory pharmacologist in the Division of Toxicology at the Bureau of Foods. The research that I was engaged in, under Dr. Taylor, involved flavoring agents.

We were doing toxicological studies on food additives, pesticides, and flavoring agents. Many of the flavoring agents were from plants such as sassafras, from which safrole was extracted. Sassafras tea was made by steeping the roots in boiling water. In addition, the root-beer industry used safrole as a flavoring agent in its product. These studies were designed to allow laboratory rats to ingest certain levels in parts-per-million (PPM) of the safrole to determine the sub-acute and chronic toxicity of these mixtures. The studies were conducted for periods from six months to two years, after which the animals were autopsied and subject to pathological examination. There were a number of studies of this type that we were involved with and that were used as models by the industry for food additives, pesticides studies, and other intentional and accidental additives.

There came a time when we got concerned about the volatility of these flavoring agents and realized also that there could possibly be a chemical reaction that could result from the mixing of these flavoring agents in a person's diet. J. B. Wilson, an organic chemist in our agency, developed techniques to extract dietary mixtures to determine the levels that were being consumed by the animals. We discovered that some of the flavors, by the very nature of their compounds, would volatilize from the diets. We were also able to discover that some of the reactions with other things in the diet produced other chemicals in the mixture.

These types of studies would establish a full career in government for me. There were certain scientific organizations with which we became affiliated where we could present our research findings and publish the results. They were organizations and publications such as *The Journal of the Official Agricultural Chemist*, and the Society of Toxicology and Pharmacology.

Each year, research scientists came from universities, corporations, government entities, and foreign countries to meet in various cities in the United States for the purpose of presenting their scientific papers. These sessions usually lasted one week with presentations being made eight to nine hours daily. The meetings were held in Atlantic City, Philadelphia, Washington, DC, and a few other cities. For the first nine years of my FDA career, I was located in the south agricultural building. This happened primarily because the agency had no building with bathrooms of its own, and because the FDA, from its inception, was an agency under the Department of Agriculture. Later, the FDA was placed under the Department of HEW, and appropriations were made that allowed the FDA to build and operate an animal laboratory at the foot of Capitol Hill.

During my first nine years at the FDA, there were also many changes coming to the city, primarily the rebuilding of the southwest quadrant of Washington, DC. This area of southwest DC was undergoing total urban renewal. The quadrant ran from the southwest waterfront east to South Capitol Street and from Independence Avenue south to M Street toward Fort McNair.

During the renewal, there were a huge number of small, private businesses that were replaced by new homes and businesses as well as new government buildings. Most of the area was leveled by bulldozers, except for a few special buildings. The United States was still trying to work its way through the Cuban Missile Crisis and the Cold War with Russia. The city was bracing itself for the demise of the streetcar system, the introduction of the subway, and the use of buses. However, neither the federal nor state government had come to grips with one of the greatest dilemmas since the Civil War. That dilemma was how to rectify the problem of second-class citizenship that had been thrust upon the largest minority group in the country, the Negroes. The battle over school desegregation had only whetted the appetite for more freedom of the Negroes in the United States. One of the most annoying of the problems for Negroes was the laws in the South, which were primarily designed to suffocate any thoughts of public-accommodation concerns, including jobs and housing. School desegregation, and later on, the open-housing laws, caused a mass movement of Caucasians away from the inner cities, a movement that was called the "white flight" to the suburbs. This phenomenon stimulated great activity for the building and real-estate industries to accommodate the wave of movement.

The assassination of President Kennedy and the installation of President Lyndon Johnson provided a new approach toward solving some of the race problems. President Johnson, although a southerner from Texas, was labeled as one of the prime movers of civil rights due to a number of laws passed during his administration with the support of the US Congress, where he had served for many years. One of these laws in 1968 addressed fair housing. This law slowed "white flight" to the suburbs because the real-estate builders and the industry, which was a part of the conspiracy to keep housing segregation alive, were under the gun to obey the law or suffer severe consequences.

In addition, the Equal Employment Opportunity (EEO) laws opened the doors for Negro real-estate agents to be hired by large realty corporations. This movement placed the Negro agents and others in strategic positions so that the Negro buyer would not be victims of steering and other covert activities designed to circumvent the law. In those areas where certain subdivisions were traditional white enclaves that had segregated schools where they felt the status quo would be maintained, the Supreme Court mandated busing to achieve racial balance.

Just as desegregation was being mandated in the military and government, private industry and corporations had to open their doors. The kicker here was effective because any business doing contracting with the federal, state, and local governments had to make affirmative action a part of their protocol in order to operate legally.

As I continued my career in the Department of Health Education and Welfare, I observed integration in the "rank and file departments" of the federal government. At the FDA, I saw a small influx of Negro scientist in the agency in the decade of the 1960s and 1970s.

Although I moved into a civilian era of employment, I still maintained an active role in the military reserves. In order to serve in the reserves, I was required to attend summer camp at a military base for a period of two weeks every year. During those years, I attended summer camps at some of the oldest and most notable camps, such as Fort Knox (where the gold is stored), Fort Campbell, and several other bases.

Quite often, I would see fellow officers from my alma mater, Hampton Institute; however, almost all of my acquaintances were Negro officers. The class instructors were usually of the "Caucasoid" persuasion. The officers that I often met at most of my camps and with whom I became good friends were from Washington, DC. Three of these friends from DC, with the last names of Carter, Balthazar, and Penn, were schoolteachers in the school system. In the summer of 1964, we were assigned for training in Georgia. I didn't like the idea of going to Georgia, so I stayed at home. Maybe I had a premonition or was being protected by my guardian angel. In any event, there was an incident that left one of my friends from DC, Lieutenant Colonel Lemuel A. Penn, dead. He had attended several camps with me, and he went to Georgia for the 1964 summer camp. On his way home, driving through Georgia at night, Penn and two US Army reservists, Charles E. Brown and John D. Howard, were with him. They were followed by an automobile, which came alongside the driver's side of the car and fired a blast from a shotgun at close range that killed Penn, who was the driver. The killers: two KKK goons by the names of Cecil Myers and Howard Sims, who were later tried and acquitted by an all-white jury. These same two were later tried in federal court for violating the civil rights of Lt. Col. Penn, and they were sentenced to six years in the federal penitentiary.

The reason I had not been south of Washington for more than twelve years before this incident was due to all of the unrest related to civil-rights activity. If I had gone, no doubt, I would have been armed and ready to shoot if provoked or attacked. During the early 1960s, I was involved in a lot of activities, including raising a family, and I ultimately decided on dropping the military duties. Much of my time was spent taking courses at the local universities to enhance my career.

The creation of the Equal Opportunity Commission under the Civil Rights Agency provided impetus to more evenly balance the scale in hiring. One of the programs directed at putting teeth into the laws enacted called for affirmative action. Each federal department was required to design a protocol, and every department and agency was required to present plans for affirmative action. The progress for action was to be reviewed on a yearly basis, and the plans were to be initiated at all levels of government. The federal government served as the best laboratory for devising and implementing such a program, mainly because of its management structure. For example, there were departments, bureaus, divisions, branches, and sections. This structure provided a clear line of supervision of all elements of government. This structure also provided a road map for corporate America, as well as for the university systems.

Many of the critics of affirmative action tried to set up roadblocks by throwing around terms such as *reverse discrimination* and *quota systems*. Many were too blind to see that all new proposals, laws, and regulations will suffer growing pains and unexpected problems that need to be rectified if they run counter to the spirit of the well-intentioned laws and regulations.

I became an EEO counselor in the late 1960s, mainly because I had firsthand experience dealing with segregation and discrimination both in the military and civilian arenas. Because my experiences were up close and personal, it made me a good candidate to participate in the program. I grew up in Georgia under the strictest of laws and regulations related to unequal opportunities. I attended segregated schools, was drafted into a segregated military service, was hired into a segregated government job, and lived in a society that showed segregation in housing, schools, and all other walks of life. I was able to offer my knowledge on how to weave one's way through the minefields of life that had been presented to me. I also took great pride in myself for being a good listener to those who came before me pleading their cases. The EEO counselor provided the first contact for the chain of events that the complainant had to face to be able to put a foot in the door to resolve his or her issues that related to discrimination practices by his or her employer.

The system required that the counselor would meet with the complainant and initiate an investigation into his or her charges of acts of discrimination against him or her by supervisors. After formally receiving the issues and taking the names of witnesses, if any, the counselor would: set an appointment to meet with the supervisor to get his or her side of the issue, meet with witnesses, and prepare a report to be passed onto the bureau EEO officer and his staff. Accompanying the report would be any documents that the counselor was given by either party. The counselor made no determination as to the veracity of the claim to support either the supervisor or the employee.

The bureau EEO and his or her staff would review the report from the counselor and determine whether it warranted further investigation. If they determined that it did, an EEO investigator would be appointed to the case. The difference between the action of the counselor and the investigator was that the investigator would place all persons testifying under oath in preparation for court action. The counselor's role would be complete at the beginning of the investigative phase of a case.

The diligence that I showed in casework as an EEO counselor was rewarded in 1974 when my FDA supervisor, Dr. Jean Taylor, recommended to the Agency EEO Committee that I be considered as a candidate for the first EEO Achievement Award issued by the Food and Drug Administration. Subsequently, I was the recipient of that award.

Throughout my career with the Food and Drug Administration, my approach to getting recommended for promotions followed a simple method. I would check the civil-service announcements that were posted periodically to see what was required for the next promotion level in my series. I would then follow all of the requirements and couple the academic pursuits to qualify. Soon, I knew how to work through the maze. Throughout the 1960s, 1970s, and into the 1980s, I made steady progress in my career development. It was quite checkered with highs and lows, but I was always moving forward.

I recall one frustrating time on my journey that was probably my worst negative interaction with a member of the establishment. My section supervisor and my branch chief recommended and forwarded a request for me to be promoted to a GS-7 pharmacologist. It passed through channels all the way to the division administrative officer who, for some illogical reason, let the request incubate in his inbox for over a year. Either my immediate supervisors did not act to pressure him to move the request, or he ignored them. I knew it was not being moved forward to the bureau because on a few occasions, when I worked overtime, I checked his office inbox. Since his office was unlocked, I had access.

Finally, after approximately fourteen months, I called the bureau chief for an appointment. When I went to his office, I gave him an account and the chronology of what had take place during that fourteen-month period. He maintained a calm attitude and promised that he would check into it. He also assured me that the request for my promotion was in his office and that it would be processed in two to four weeks.

Within two weeks, I was pleasantly surprised to receive information that my promotion had been processed. I examined the paperwork, and to my surprise, the title on the promotion was incorrect in that it was a promotion to a GS-7 biologist. This change had been made by the administrative officer without consultation with my immediate supervisors. I went back to the bureau chief and challenged the title to be reclassified into a GS-7 pharmacologist based on the original application.

To accept the biology rating, I would have lost approximately $500 to $1,000 dollars per year. The reason was that the pharmacologist was a short-category position, and the pharmacology position got an added monetary premium to enhance recruiting of pharmacologists. Eventually, my request was honored, and I got the position as the first Negro pharmacologist ever hired or promoted in the FDA. From the GS-7 position on up the scale, I did not experience any more major problems from anyone in the FDA.

The movement toward the top positions was unchallenged mainly because most of the weight for being promoted was based on the research and the acceptance of research that I published in scientific journals. In addition, at the level of GS-11 to GS-13, my title was changed to a supervisory pharmacologist. These positions also required scientists to develop and outline protocols for studies and a requirement to review food-additive petitions. In addition to developing study protocols, the scientists were responsible for supervising the lower-grade- level scientists who were conducting laboratory animal studies and coordinating the work with other lab specialists. The other lab units were data processing and statistical units, hematology units, analytical chemical units, and pathology units. These studies were most important because they formed the basis for developing protocols and making decisions relative to the safety of food additives.

Those of us that were college and university graduates were aware that roads leading to our success had always been totally unpaved, rutted, invisible, and usually lead to a dead end. Therefore, when we had a limited amount of success, we looked around to see and determine how we could help our brothers who were less educated and less fortunate than ourselves. Many of these were government employees working at the very lowest level who were not motivated and who felt that no one cared.

Like most Negroes who had witnessed the civil-rights activities that were initiated by modern-day "Davids" like Martin Luther King, Rosa Parks, Bayard Rustin, Thurgood Marshall, and others, I felt that all of us should band together to help the less fortunate. I was aware that I was not in that large arena, but I could make some moves in my little pond. One of these opportunities presented itself in my agency. We were all aware that we had a large pool of lower-level employees with limited opportunities to qualify for promotions. We also noted that many of these were young Negro youth who were also trying to raise families on inadequate incomes. We felt that our laboratories could serve as an ideal place to do something that was unique and provide some motivation to some of our downtrodden brothers and sisters. Many of these workers never completed high school. We knew that the areas in which they needed to be tutored were reading and math. Several scientists in my bureau joined with some program directors to help these workers to obtain GED certificates. We set up the program and encouraged them to take their one-hour lunch program in which we would all bring our brown paper bags and they would spend that time with us learning to read and understand math. In general, it was designed to help them to pass the GED program.

They could then become more proficient assistants to the laboratory scientists. We felt that we could teach them to weigh and measure materials for animal diets. In addition, we could, by utilizing a hands-on approach, get them involved in other lab procedures, such as recording data and record-keeping. We were very pleased that we had some success, which was indicated by the fact that a few of these people had impressed their supervisors with their newfound skills, which lead to them receiving promotions.

I wish that I could state truthfully that all of my efforts were successful, but that was not the case. I got involved with another group who felt that we could formulate a plan that would be beneficial to ex-prisoners. Some of these people would work in the labs on a one-on-one, student-to-mentor basis. I was introduced to a member of the Washington, DC school board who was sponsoring the program in conjunction with the prison-reform system. I should've been skeptical about the program's operation, but I was willing to try to help. After I agreed to help, I was called to an FBI office to meet with my student and to get an orientation about the program and the participant. The FBI officer questioned this ex-prisoner for several hours about his background. They started with his first run-in with the legal system. The officer informed the person that he was to verify everything that they legally had on him as a part of his record. I never knew why this was done, but he apparently answered everything adequately and satisfactorily to the agent.

The program required him to work twenty hours each week with me and to spend twenty hours in school at the University of the District of Columbia (UDC). By doing this, he was paid for a forty-hour week. The program was to be certified by the University of DC, and all enrollees were to be physically in attendance at UDC beginning at the first semester of each year. I demanded accountability for his attendance at school as well as at work. I wanted a schedule of all of his classes and a weekly work schedule. This individual turned out to be a con artist par excellence. He did not want me to know his itinerary. He was a recovering drug addict on the methadone program. I soon discovered that he had acquired a new addiction, or habit: drinking whiskey. When I became convinced that he was not only drinking but also lying and not being honest and accountable, I decided to sever the ties. When I reported him to his counselor, he swore I was lying about him, not treating him with respect, and other accusations. I then demanded that he be removed from my lab. He was removed, and that completed my experiment with humans; I continued with my "predictable" animals.

Probably one of the most interesting tasks that I was assigned to perform came late in my career. The FDA had major concerns about animal-laboratory conditions that might compromise the results of laboratory studies. These concerns centered on the condition of the housing facilities, sanitization, animal husbandry and health of the animals, protocols, cross-contamination, record-keeping, and so forth. A course of study called "good laboratory animal practices" was developed in the agency. A number of scientists and inspectors were assigned to a school in Pine Bluff, Arkansas, to take a comprehensive course in good laboratory practices. At the completion of the courses, teams comprised of scientists and inspectors working together were sent to the lab-animal facilities of major pharmaceutical companies where studies were being conducted on products that were destined to come before the FDA for approval. These labs welcomed the teams and were very cooperative when they were slated for inspections.

These inspections enabled the review scientists to develop great respect and learn a lot about their peers in the corporate world. Prior to these connections, we often had contact with many of them at scientific meetings that were of common interest to us. I was involved in doing laboratory inspections at several firms and then resumed my activities in my own lab.

CHAPTER X

The Setting Sun on My FDA Career and the Beginning of a New Life: Retirement

WHEN THE YEAR 1982 arrived, I began to review my life and to analyze my future endeavors. I had spent approximately forty years in a variety of arenas.

These were some of the realistic things that confronted me:

- After high school, I was drafted into the military for two and a half years.
- After my release from the military, I went to college and graduated after four years.
- I returned to the army for two years.
- I spent thirty years as a federal employee.
- Two of my children had graduated from college and gotten married.

Just about this time, I realized that further advancement was not likely, so it was time for me to retire and start a new career.

I researched several career options, and I decided to take a course and become a realtor. Several months before retiring, I passed the real-estate exams and was qualified as a realtor. Following retirement, I went to work for Nyman Realtor Company, later, for ERA Nyman Realty, and then for Coldwell Banker Stevens Brokerage.

At approximately fifty-eight years of age, I launched into a new career that I felt would be fairly lucrative and exciting; however, like every new situation, there was a game within the game. This new career venture required me to learn the realty game from the bottom up. The learning process included information about zoning laws, titling, special coding, and much more. The business I found was fun and lucrative when you knew the answers to questions presented by your clients. I soon developed a style that paid off handsomely. I insisted that all of my clients, both buyers and sellers, receive my real-estate orientation, which would last from one to two hours. I would give them information about real estate, both buying and selling, so that they would feel comfortable as they traveled through the minefield of either buying or selling. I covered financing, appraising, tiling, home inspections, termite inspections, home styles, and so forth.

Over a period of twenty-five years, I have sold several hundred houses, lots, and commercial properties. My area of work in both Prince George's (PG) County and Washington, DC, primarily covered homes sold and purchased by low- to middle-income families. In these particular areas, a good agent needed to know a lot about innovative financing as well as how to work with clients who did not have a lot of money, or often, good credit ratings. These conditions made me a more knowledgeable realtor and an angel of mercy to my clients.

Once again, I had a great mentor, my manager, Donald Frederick. Because of his teaching and training and my ability to learn fast, I learned and became, in short order, an outstanding realtor. Throughout a period of more than twenty years as a realtor, I have been eligible for the top awards given by the board of realtors in both Maryland and the District of Columbia. Each year, the top producers were featured at a banquet, and the awards were presented to the eligible recipients. My brokerage company also gave company awards to their outstanding agents. To receive a PG County or DC Board award, an agent was required to have a year's production of more than $1.5 million in sold and settled properties. For my total twenty-plus years in real estate, I have always qualified for the company and board awards.

If one were to take a house that is approximately thirty-five feet long and multiply that by four hundred houses sold, one would have a total distance of fourteen thousand feet, equating to approximately two and a half miles. So, if these houses were placed side by side, the distance covered would be more than two and a half miles of homes sold and settled.

Working and earning the extra money as a realtor allowed me to engage in a number of things that I would not have been able to afford on my retirement income alone. For an example, it provided some luxuries for the children that we still had in college; this was especially true for Billy and Gerald, who owned their own cars for traveling back and forth to college and to work.

My activities at the agency and in real estate included more than all work and no play. Many of the government departments had athletic programs with an athletic director. The only program that I took any interest in was the HEW Bowling League. I had never bowled, but I joined to get the exercise, which also brought out my competitive spirit. I was thirty-nine or forty years old, but I quickly learned the fundamentals of the game. Once I committed to the league, I bought equipment such as shoes, ball, and bag. In addition, I started watching the pros on television, and I bought books to study the game.

I participated in duckpin bowling for one year and then switched to ten-pin. Bowling houses were, like many other activities in the area, located outside of Washington, DC proper, and were off-limits to Negro bowlers. Two corporations controlled the bowling in this particular area: Bowl America and Fair Lanes. The equipment for the house featured two companies: Brunswick and AMF. Both were national chains. The

Bowl America Corporation was a local one owned by a Mr. Goldberg, whose first bowling establishment was on Cameron Street in Bethesda, Maryland. He parlayed that into a chain of bowling houses around or near the beltway. A few of these houses were available for Negroes to bowl and have league activities. For a long number of years, the Masons in DC owned a bowling house on Tenth Street near U Street. Some black bowlers belonged who were also members of the National Bowling Association (NBA). The NBA sponsored tournaments for Negro bowlers who were members of that association. Participants came from DC, Philadelphia, New York, Chicago, Detroit, Saint Louis, and a few other major cities mostly in the Midwest.

One of the major bowling houses for the Bowl America chain was located in the newly redeveloped southwest quadrant of DC at M Street and Third Street. Government leagues began to have their games in this house in the southwest area, and it was the house of choice because of the nondiscriminatory position that was mandated by the Federal Athletic Association.

Bowling houses that ringed the beltway (Bowl America and Fair Lanes) did not allow open bowling or league bowling for Negroes. The American Bowling Congress (ABC) tournaments were held in the beltway houses, which prevented Negroes from participating. Even those who were ABC members of the southwest bowling center were not allowed to engage in the tournaments.

Eventually, a committee was formed from the government-league bowlers to challenge the segregation found in the Bowl America houses. The group included several professors from Howard University who bowled in our league, and I participated. At that time, I was the secretary of the HEW bowling league.

One committee member from the Sociology Department at Howard, John Staggers, was appointed to meet with Mr. Goldberg to negotiate the issue of the desegregation of his bowling establishments. Mr. Staggers was selected because he was a well-known, respected, and intelligent civil-rights activist. None of us were surprised when he returned from a lunch engagement with the owner, Mr. Goldberg, and one of his special corporate officers, Sylvester Sobanski, with good news.

Mr. Goldberg drafted a letter to all of his bowling houses that Negroes were to be welcomed to open bowling, league bowling, and tournament bowling anytime in all of his houses. Needless to say, the Fair Lane houses and all others instituted the same policy. We soon saw Negroes being hired as workers and managers in many of the area bowling establishments. Bowling provided, for me, some of the most exciting, yet relaxing times of my life, and I bowled competitively for more than thirty-five years.

My bowling involvement included my becoming active in the Youth Bowling Arena. I became a bowling instructor in a youth bowling league. All youth bowlers were required to meet at certain bowling establishments every Saturday morning from about 9:00 a.m. to 1:00 p.m. The youth ranged in age from about nine to twenty-one years old. They received individual instruction at every level. They were grouped as follows: eight to ten years old, eleven to thirteen years old, fifteen to eighteen years old, and nineteen to twenty-one years old. They competed in league activities according to their age groups, and in addition, we would carry them to various youth tournaments held throughout the bowling season.

These types of engagements trained those young individuals to be good citizens; even though the competition was very keen, they learned to be sportsmen. They learned to recognize the talents found in their fellow bowlers. They understood and appreciated the efforts presented by their coaches. They accepted being disciplined and understood that any breach could eliminate them from the program. So, "order" was the order of the day.

One summer, after the yearly bowling schedule had been completed, I received information about a professional bowling camp designed to train youth bowlers. The site was in Canton, Ohio, and it was run by two professional tour bowlers, Fred Jaske and Wayne Zahn. Both had been on the pro-bowlers tour and had been on national television, and they were from our bowling league. I transported my two sons, Billy and Gerald, and the two sons of two close friends, David Bailey and Elliott Robertson. We spent one week in Canton with the youth members bowling all day, every day from approximately 9:00 a.m. to 9:00 p.m. They were all housed in the bowling alley itself, sleeping, eating, and socializing together for that whole week.

Interestingly, when I arrived with my four charges, we were the only minorities (Negroes) in the camp; however, during that week, there was no racial tension, nor were there incidents that ever reared their ugly heads. All of us were well received by the bowling staff, the management, and all of the youth bowlers.

Beginning after their enrollment on a Sunday night, each student was filmed as he bowled. At the end of the week, each individual was taped again to see how much he had improved in his bowling game. In order for every bowler to receive individual attention and training, they bowled in shifts. While one shift was bowling, the other two shifts were playing outside on the basketball court or the tennis court. From the outset, each bowler was given a composition book for instructions to be recorded by the coach. Notations included progress or techniques that required extra training or techniques that needed to be practiced. The professional coaches and I got to be well acquainted with each other. They both learned that I was a youth bowling instructor, and so, they asked me to participate in the training of the other youth bowlers. It was a very exciting week for all who participated, and I feel that we all hated to see it end. Each bowler received a certificate for the completion of the program.

When we returned to Washington, DC, Billy, Gerald, and their friends resumed their bowling activity with their league, and in addition, they began to participate in a number of the local bowling tournaments. Over the next five or six years, they won a huge number of trophies in team and individual categories, to the surprise of many of their peers and coaches.

When Billy and Gerald finished high school and entered college, they put a hold on their participation in bowling. Both Billy and Gerald got employment in different arenas, and bowling was still on hold until they later joined some of the leagues in the metropolitan area. Billy pursued bowling only for a short period of time and never fully reached his potential in the bowling arena. Gerald, on the other hand, had become highly competitive in the game of bowling. So much so that he began not only to participate in league bowling but also in "pot bowling," where he won a substantial amount of money. His league performance also went to the top, with him having bowling averages up over the 220s. It was during this time that he bowled, over a period of several years, three hundred games and several eight hundred-scratch sets. He won several national single tournaments, winning his highest award of $8,000.

During the late 1990s, Gerald, Billy, and I, along with two other friends, formed a five-man team in Alexandria, Virginia. The league members were all aware that we were a father-son team and were bowling respectfully in a scratch league. We bowled for a couple of years together until Billy's job called him out of town.

Gerald got married to Candy Mason in May 2004. The marriage was considered to be a successful venture for both, and the family acquired another bowler. Gerald proceeded in assisting Candy in perfecting her game. She was successful immediately because she participated in the National Amateur Bowlers Incorporated (NABI) tournaments alongside Gerald. She won several tournaments in NABI and also won second place in a major tournament in Las Vegas, Nevada, which netted approximately $4,000. The two of them, bowling in mixed doubles, also won a couple of league championships.

CHAPTER XI

Lazy, Hazy 'Daze' of Summer

ASIDE MY INTEREST IN bowling, I decided to fulfill a dream that I had from early childhood. At a very early age, my father introduced me to fishing in the Flint River in my hometown, Albany. As I sat on the banks of the river, I observed boaters fishing in the middle of the river. This river ran through our town and separated the east side from the west, and the counties around Albany boasted of several creeks and lakes. The river also provided hydroelectric power for the cities and counties surrounding Albany. My fishing expos started when I was approximately six or seven years old. A lot of fisherman used canoes and flat-paddles; however, some who could afford it had motors for their boats. The river was very rocky, so no large boats or yachts were seen. Most of the fish that we caught were carp, catfish, bream, eels, and sunfish. Generally speaking, most of the seafood that we ate was trucked in from Florida. I always felt that one could catch more fish from a boat than from the banks, so I yearned for the day when I could realize one of my favorite dreams.

At the age of forty-eight, one of my friends, Buffington Falls, bought a boat, and he and I went out on the Potomac River in DC and enjoyed the day immensely. His boat was docked at Bowling AFB along with a number of other boaters. One day, he told me there was a boat for sale that I might like and that the price was reasonable. In 1971, I contacted the owner and we made a deal, and my boating life began. The boat that was for sale was a 1958 Owens single-engine craft. It was twenty-two feet long with a small cuddy cabin that slept two people. The boat's name was *Lady Theta*. I renamed her by christening her the *Lady Lynn*. My daughters, Valerie and Melba, had the middle names of Lynette and Lynn. The whole boat had to be reconditioned, and this challenge provided a learning process that served me well throughout my boating career. I had the boat for only a short period of time when I determined that reconditioning was in order, to include installing a new engine. I worked on that boat for two of three summers before I was satisfied that it was seaworthy. The work required removing all of the paint down to the bare wood. Later came rebedding; recaulking; removing and replacing brass screws; installing new cushions; and installing a new propeller, compass, bilge pump, radio, and depth finder. At least two weeks of every summer for several years was spent in dry dock reconditioning my prize-winning boat.

Geri, my wife, was not enthusiastic about boating, primarily because her father, Arthur Hooper, drowned while working on a fishing boat. So, she was very uncomfortable with the idea of becoming a boater. Therefore, in my early boating experience, she participated sparingly. The first few years of activity on the water were primarily with my two sons, Billy and Gerald, who appeared to be fearless.

Most of the boating that we were engaged in for several years was up and down the Potomac and Anacostia Rivers, as well as on the Washington Channel down to the Woodrow Wilson Bridge and back. For the first long-distance trip that I took, Billy and I left Washington and traveled via the Potomac River to Callao, Virginia, with a trip to Cobb Island in Maryland and back to Washington. After a few years as owners of the small *Lady Lynn.*, disaster struck. The boat, due to a leak in the exhaust system, sank at the dock in the Pentagon Lagoon Marina. Subsequently, it was raised, and the damage was assessed. I then decided that the cost to refurbish would possibly cost more than the boat was worth.

I went to the Washington Marina and discussed the situation with a salesman who made a deal with me that allowed me to trade in my boat for another. The boat for which I traded was a 1972 fiberglass, twenty-eight-foot, twin-engine pacemaker that slept six passengers comfortably, and it was the boat of my dreams. After owning it for a few months, I discovered some overheating-engine problems. I went back to Washington Marina and ordered two new Marine engines. I was now ready to roll! I personally refurbished the interior with wood and carpeting to give the interior a classy appearance.

I also became dissatisfied with the marinas in the metropolitan Washington area, so I took the new boat and berthed it at Olverson's Marina in Callao, Virginia. This was an ideal location because it was located a few miles from the Chesapeake Bay and the great fishing area of the Potomac River. In addition, many of the rendezvous that my squadron was engaged in were only a few miles from the marina location in which many of the Northern Virginia Power Squadron members also had their boats located. Also, one great feature that this marina had was that all boat slips were undercover, with both electricity and water at the dock.

I envisioned my family and I enjoying many summer days on the water; however, I had to do some serious learning, because I soon found out that operating a boat requires more skills than operating a car. Boats are not equipped with brakes; in addition, one sees the effect on steering boats from elements such as wind, waves, tides, and speed. Boat steering is very difficult, especially when reversing. Single engines with single propellers have a tendency to back toward port (left). So, even if you turned the wheel properly, you just increase the power to force it to back to starboard (right). Twin engines with twin props are much easier to back to either port or starboard. Navigating is fairly easy in rivers and creeks where you can see shore to shore; however, one must be careful of operating in waters too shallow for fear of grounding or striking submerged objects and then sinking. There are other hazards too numerous to mention.

As soon as I bought the first boat, the *Lady Lynn*, I decided to take a boating course. It was called Piloting and required four to six months of intensive studying. I passed the course, which was being offered by a private organization called The Power Squadron. The squadron offered more courses for the public and its members than the coast guard offered. The squadron offered only the boating course to nonmembers in the public. Membership in the boating organization was strictly by invitation.

The Northern Virginia Power Squadron accepted me in the class, and I passed; however, the nominating committee for membership created quite a dilemma for the squadron, as a whole, by offering me membership in the squadron. Later, a prominent member told me that a very heated verbal debate took place upon my nomination. The problem that they'd had centered on the fact that the organization had never sanctioned the inclusion of a minority, for the squadron had no minorities as members before me. There were several other power squadrons in the metropolitan Washington area, such as the Potomac River Power Squadron, The Rockville Power Squadron, the Dundalk, and The Patuxent River Power Squadron, none of which had accepted a person of color as a member. Once I became a member, I took other courses in the squadron such as Seamanship and Communications (Radio, Radar, and Signaling), and became knowledgeable about navigation, marine-engine maintenance, advanced piloting, and so forth.

Once you became a member, you were expected to work on committees and perform a number of duties as a teacher or an assistant. The management structure of the organization consisted of "the bridge." There were:

1) Commander
2) Executive Officer

3) Administrative Officer
4) Assistant Administrative Officer
5) Secretary
6) Treasurer
7) Chaplin

The commander served one year, and the executive was usually voted to the command spot. The same process followed, having the administrative officer move up to executive, and the assistant administrative officer up to administrative officer. A new assistant administrator would be voted onto "the bridge" to complete the true bridge command. The secretary and the treasurer often served their positions for more than one term.

Meetings were held one night every month. There were other special activities and water functions that were held throughout the year. There were power and sail squadrons throughout most of the states and US possessions. National meetings were held once a year. Most of the time, they were held in Miami and in some other Florida cities.

The National Power Squadron Organization consisted of fifty districts. These districts follow the numbering of the naval districts where they were located. The Northern Virginia Power Squadron, along with many other power squadrons on the east coast of the United States, was in District Five. Some of the major events in my squadron were Founder's Day, The Change of Watch, D-5 conferences, the Christmas party, and summer programs, which were often on-the-water activities. These were called "rendezvous" and featured boating activities as well as cookouts held at marinas. These were usually held June through August. Our boats traveled from Washington, DC, Maryland, and Virginia, over some of the major tributaries (rivers and creeks that flow into the Chesapeake Bay).

On Sundays at these rendezvous, boats took part in navigation contests. A course was laid out with five to six legs going in different directions, and the boats raced against the clock. Each boat had a captain (who was the pilot), a navigator, and a timekeeper. In addition, a person who was not a member of the crew served as an official observer. His job was to see that all rules were followed according to the squadron regulations. For an example, no boat was to cross the starting line before the timer fired his gun, no course packages were to be opened until the race started, and all time clocks were to be turned off as the boat entered the last leg of the race.

These contests were well organized for the contestants. A trophy was given to the first three boats finishing the course. There were five or more contests held every year, on the water, by the squadron. At the end of the year, a boat was declared the winner if it participated in at least three contests and clocked an average winning time for the three races that was better than that of all other boats. The boat then received the Boat of the Year honors.

I went to the Northern Virginia Power Squadron (NVPS) to learn more about boating and stayed with the organization for more than thirty years. During that time, I enjoyed every moment. I took an interest and participated in all of the activities. Being in an organization that was a part of a national group was a great experience for me. During all of the activities, both local and district meetings, I was the only minority present. I grew accustomed to seeing that scenario over and over, so I was not overwhelmed by the situation. I had my family come and participate in many of our local meetings, especially my wife. I held every bridge position except treasurer and received high marks from my peers in the organization.

One position, secretary, gave me my first major assignment, which was organizing and conducting the Founder's Day festivities. All members of the bridge wore their uniforms on this and other special occasions, as well as at other monthly meetings. I outlined a special memorial service on Founder's Day to honor all deceased members. It was very unique because we lit, and later extinguished, each candle with a roll call of each deceased member with a tapping of a bell after the extinguishing of the candle. My trumpet-playing son, Gerald, played taps at the end of the extinguishing of the last candle. We saw a number of members shedding tears as they were overcome by their emotions.

The everyday part of the secretarial job was record-keeping, property storage and maintenance, and preparing the minutes of the meetings. I worked as a secretary for two years. Following the second year, the selection committee chose me for the job of assistant administrative officer, which consisted of chairing several committees. The big job here was to select sites for rendezvous and assist in operation of the contest. I worked for two years as an administrative officer.

My next position, executive officer, began my preparation to become the commander of the squadron. In 1985, after one year as the executive officer, I was then elected commander of the NVPS.

It was an exciting time and the First Lady, Geri, and I really put on an outstanding performance during our year in office. We attended all of the national and district functions and were always aware that we were being observed with wonderment. We discovered later that no African-American had ever been a squadron commander of any squadron of the United States. Although we were under the watchful eyes of everyone whenever and wherever we traveled, we were always received graciously and with the utmost respect. The members of our squadron, and of our district, were very pleased and proud of us.

CHAPTER XII

The Greatest Assets of My Life

I HAVE CALCULATED THE value of many things that I have owned: boats, cars, a home, real-estate assets, and so forth. And none have the value of my deceased wife, four children, and four grandchildren. Beginning with the first one, and through the whole tribe, my wife and I have had many hours of joy, jubilation, happiness, and proud moments at their various and sundry accomplishments and antics, which provided, for us, many euphoric moments.

Each child has given us something special to be proud of. It did not have to be a Nobel Prize or other great achievements. Often, it was speaking a first word or taking the first step, or performing for us before an audience. My statement was always, "That's my daughter (or son, or grandchild)."

They, too, were fortunate in having parents who cared. We cared enough to train them and discipline them, so they understood that *our way* would serve them no matter what parts of the world they traveled. Our way might go against the grain of the present idiocy, but we believed that to spare the rod was to spoil the child. They had to be made aware that challenges would be coming to them in every arena in which they would choose to compete. My definition is to provide discipline, which did include moderate spanking (contrary to the Dr.

Spock utilization of the book approach). We spanked our children only when all of the other approaches did not get results, and never with objects that would inflict injury. Often, an open hand across the derriere would suffice. Most of the time punishment was a solitary period of standing in the corner of a room for a period of time to allow the child to realize the error of his or her ways.

Our children were taught to love and respect, and our love would be returned four-fold. All of them were showered with love and kindness from both parents. They were always rewarded if they showed proper behavior and kindness as well as proper respect for the elderly. Birthdays and Christmas were special occasions, and gifts were given during those times.

As our children reached their pubescence in their childhood, we, as a couple, were aware and recognized that gender concerns needed to be dealt with in a special way. We had the mother dealing with motherly guidance to the girls and the father dealing with specific issues that related primarily to the father and the boys. There were female subjects dealing with mother to daughter, and there were male subjects dealing with father to son; however, I, as the father, gave my daughters the practical lessons of conduct that we adhered to relative to courtship.

These matters had to do with the conduct of the couple that was acceptable to us as parents. For example, any male that visited with our daughters and who planned to take them out on a date had to follow our dictates relative to conduct. First, they had to come to our daughters' home and be introduced to their parents. My role as the father took on special meaning at this introduction: with my daughter not being present, I introduced my wife and myself to the suitor. In addition, we asked for some information about who he was, who his parents were and where he came from, along with other pertinent information that we deemed important to know. We asked for parents' names, addresses, telephone numbers, and so forth, where the young man was attending school, and his goals in life.

Next on the agenda was a lecture on his respect for both of us and for our daughters. First, he was to understand that he must, at all times, come to her home to pick her up to go out on a date with the understanding that she was to be returned to the same location and make sure that she entered the house before he departed, and that there also would be a curfew time and no dates during the school week. He was to understand that we were concerned about her future life, and for us, that meant that a child was not in her immediate future and we were not ready to be grandparents.

We further helped him to understand that our family was interested in giving her an opportunity to organize a career, which included college graduation. This same lecture was also given when the boys arrived at a certain age as they approached and dated young women.

During the course of their teenage time of life, due to them going away to college in Virginia, they were allowed to have a couple of parties sponsored by us at our home. These parties would have special supervision by us. The maximum number of guests to be invited to the party would be only twenty people. Our daughters were to get the message out that only people invited would be allowed to come to the party. We knew that the best way to get the communiqué out to all interested was to have my daughters issue the notice through "the grapevine," and so it was. Further, as they arrived at the house, we laid out ground rules that consumption of alcoholic beverages, smoking, and using illegal drugs would be strictly prohibited at the party. At least one of the parents, usually me, as the father, would be the greeter of all of the invited guests. Time of arrival for guests would be 8:30 p.m., and the time for departure would be no later than 12:30 a.m. When the lights were blinked on and off, guests were expected to depart—immediately!

I am very happy that I have lived to see them perform masterfully no matter the challenge. In addition to meeting the challenges and class situations and other world situations, they were expected to love, learn, and deal with their fellow human travelers. Most of all, they were to understand that all of us were not endowed with the same talents;

however, everyone has the ability to contribute something to the well-being of mankind.

As of 2009, my youngest child was forty-five years old, and not one of my children has been a disappointment to their mother and me. All of them passed through the difficult period as teenagers without being a disciplinary problem, running afoul of the law, going to jail, dropping out of school, smoking, drinking excessively, engaging in drug activity, having children out of wedlock, and many of the behaviors frowned on by society.

My four children all attended and graduated from college. Ironically, they all chose to go to the alma mater of their parents, Hampton Institute and University. Life after college found them gainfully employed in the fields of their choosing. They work as a team to solve all family problems. For an example, one of the most difficult periods came near the end of March 2003 when my wife, their mother, was stricken with a massive stroke and was in a coma and a state of vegetation for more than twenty-four hours. There came a point at which a life-and-death decision had to be made by the family. Following a consultation with the doctors and medical specialists, the family was asked to make a final decision. The decision was centered on the fact that all that could be done for Geri had been done, and there was no further hope of anything that would bring her back to life. At that time, the life-support equipment was the only thing that was active, because her systems had all ceased to function on their own. The interim minister of Pennsylvania Avenue Baptist Church, Reverend Singleton, the former pastor, Revered Haggray, and our other church supporters joined with us in prayer. The children and I made the final decision to allow the medical staff to perform their last act of mercy and to release her into the hands of God Almighty.

My children showed their mettle when they, without my participation, made all of the arrangements for the wake, the funeral, and later, for their mother's internment. Their effort was also seen when they contacted her peers, lifelong friends, and relatives, so that her wake and funeral was with the accompaniment of the largest crowd of people

I've ever seen at a funeral service. This gave rise to my feeling that she was the greatest person that I have ever known or will know during my lifetime.

All of our children were always encouraged to do their best whether they were in school or pursuing a vocation or avocation. They proceeded at their own pace. They were all given a choice to participate in activities of their choosing, whether being cheerleaders, bowlers, or, in Gerald's case, an accomplished musician from elementary school to college and beyond. We probably spent more time with Gerald for two reasons: 1) he was the last child to leave the nest, and 2) his talents were exhibited worldwide because he was an exemplary trumpet player in the Washington DC area. He is still well known and invited to play in conce   many special services. The
crowing   orchestra peers came in his
senior yea   usic festival in Greece and
Yugoslavi

It was   tudents and parents as we
worked to   I chaired the fundraising
committee, and we used every idea at   posal to raise thousands of dollars to cover the entire trip there and back. We sold candy, cookies, grapefruits, and tangelos, engraved shirts, and did anything that we thought would give us a profit. We had help from the Coolidge High School faculty, staff, and principal. One city radio disc jockey and his bosses provided airtime to plug our fundraiser, which helped us to get over the top. Near the end, we were still a little short of our goal, and our faithful parents ponied up the rest. A great time was had by all who participated and made that endeavor a success.

Any discussion about the youth orchestra without giving credit to the most important person, the founder and conductor, Lynn McClain, would be ludicrous. He was the champion for the cause of all musically talented students. Through school-board action, he was allowed to petition all elementary and junior high teachers to search for musical talent at their schools. These students attended special music classes and sessions at Coolidge High School. Mr. McClain received professional help that worked with students as certain instrument professional specialists.

For an example, Gerald and his trumpet section worked with Mr. Wayne Cameron, who was a member of the Peabody Conservatory of Music and also played in the Baltimore Symphony Orchestra. As with many symphony groups, each student was constantly put to the test by having to compete by auditioning for a chair (one through four). For these teachers, the students were required to practice, practice, and practice some more. The orchestra talents were often showcased by them having to perform before a large number of music critics in places like the Kennedy Center, Carter Baron Theater, and Lisner Auditorium at George Washington University, to name a few. Gerald auditioned and won positions in the Maryland all-state, all-star band and other competitive venues.

The group of musicians that played in the DC youth orchestra during Gerald's tenure have each made their mark among their peers in the world of music. Several are playing professionally with jazz bands, and one of his closest trumpet-playing friends, Kevin Dines, is making a career by being a member of one of the top naval bands in the DC area.

After he graduated from college, he decided to attend the Virginia Commonwealth University Medical School. We were aware of the cost, but Geri and I always promised our children that if they wanted to get an advanced degree or prepare for a special profession, we would be there to aid financially and would be supportive to the best of our ability. I had retired from my government job and started another career as a real-estate agent, so help was available.

Gerald decided after one year that medical school was too stressful. When he left medical school, he had several jobs working at laboratories, clinics, and hospitals. It was during this time when he met Candy, and they became a serious couple. They often worked at the same job sites. After a while, Gerald got a job at Merck Pharmaceuticals. He moved on later to Bristol Myers and located near his job in Frederick, Maryland, where he bought a townhouse. After living there for several years, he invited Candy to join him in holy matrimony.

The wedding in 2004 was a thing of beauty following a whirlwind of preparation for the ultimate affair. Both sides of the family saw this union as an exciting one that had been made in heaven. Most of the family members, however, felt that the couple had procrastinated too long. The two began to prepare for their togetherness in earnest. They bought a new home, and shortly thereafter sold both his townhouse and her house. These two transactions stabilized their financial standings to the "nth" degree. Both Candy and Gerald had good jobs with great earning power that allowed them to set sail in a manner that would be envied by the wealthy and ne'er to do well. I was extremely proud of what they both had accomplished as a young couple.

I have reserved a special place in my heart and in my life for all of my grandchildren, and I love them all. However, a number of factors are present that prevent my spending of equal amounts of time with all of them.

Craig A. Stafford II, born on August 17, 1988, is the oldest grandson, and both Geri and I spent an inordinate amount of time with him as he grew into a teenager. We helped in transporting him to and from the babysitter, to school and back, to church, to his job at Starbucks and other activities. Both Billy and Gerald played a major role in the transportation project. The person who was his official, unofficial, mentor, guru, and personal overseer was his grandmother, Geri. After he became a teenager, he was with her in shopping centers, school activities, and especially church services. Geri's primary goal was to prepare Craig for college, primarily Hampton University, and she did an outstanding job!

When she passed, I felt that my role was changed somewhat, in that I was obligated to try to carry on with some of her most cherished wishes. The major one came true in August 2006 when Craig enrolled as a freshman at Hampton University, our family alma mater. We will make every effort to help him through so that her final dream will come true and she will continue to rest in peace.

Geri and I spent a few years involved with Craig because of some changes in his family circle. His mother, Melba, and Craig Sr. separated and later divorced. Although the divorce took place, Craig was not totally affected, because the two parents worked to assure that his interests would always be at the forefront of all major decisions made by them. During a period, he spent a week at a time with each parent; however, there came a period when he was in high school, which was near his mother's house, when he lived with her. Craig always showed his love and respect for both parents, as they were always available and eager to solve his problems, which were few. He also maintained a good relationship with the relatives of both his parents.

I am proud of his accomplishments thus far and expect he will continue on his present path and have a great and prosperous future.

Valerie met Ron while she was at Hampton, and they got married shortly after they finished college. Shortly thereafter, they went to Houston, Texas, where they both continued to pursue their education. She later received a master's degree in urban planning from Rice University. Ron received his degree in law. When they returned to the DC area, they both launched into special careers. She developed her special skills in photography and became quite a photo professional doing weddings, political affairs, retirements, and other group activities.

In addition, she was employed by the National Football League Players Association (NFLPA), a job that she ultimately became disenchanted with, primarily because of the management style of its leader. This dissatisfaction led to her filing a discrimination complaint with the federal EEOC against the organization and the administration. She was successful at winning the case and was finally compensated on the basis of the charges. She later returned to the NFLPA job site. Prior to her returning, I had a conversation with her relative to what she might encounter once she returned to the job. My reason for discussing that with her was that I was aware of a number of cases in which the employee returned to his or her formal job following the successful resolution of the case.

It was generally conceded that bad blood might have been established between the employee and his employers. This feeling would be natural because there had been an altercation and, as usual, a winner and a loser. The fathers of the development of the EEO program recognized that human nature might prevail over good intentions; therefore, many of the employers conceivably would react with some form of retaliation and harassment based on the outcome of the ruling in favor of the employee. The laws and regulations included punishment for any employer who retaliated against or harassed an EEO complainant whose case was settled in favor of the employee.

Valerie complained of just such action that began as soon as she was rehired. The earliest indication was a virtual lockout from the job site that began initially with her not receiving a key to enter the job site, which caused her to call the front desk to make entry on the job each day.

I had forewarned her that such behavior was likely to begin as soon as she reentered the job site. My statement at that time was that my approach to a situation in which I had been compensated was to seek employment elsewhere. Ultimately, my admonition to her fell on deaf ears, and she went back. Soon after she arrived on the job, she realized that my experience with these types of problems and my educated guess would come to fruition. The director of the NFLPA and his cohorts soon developed what they considered enough evidence against her to warrant a warning and ultimately expulsion from the job. It culminated in that action shortly after the death of Geri. From Valerie's complaint, it appears that they charged her with "absence without official leave" (AWOL).

Valerie's husband, Ron, passed the bar exam and began working as a legal professional in the DC courts. Throughout their thirty-plus years together, Val and Ron have made great strides both in their personal and community lives. They moved into Prince George's County and lived in one of the most prestigious areas, Mitchellville. They have two children: Ronald Jr., born on February 27, 1992, and Kyra, born on October 26, 1996. Ronnie is an astute young man, and we expect him to continue to develop. Kyra is also quite an astute young lady and will do quite well in the future.

The crowning touch came a little over two years ago when a heavenly package and a great bundle of joy, was delivered to Gerald and Candy on May 22, 2005. She was named Gabrielle Alana Jones, or Gabby. She was born approximately two years after the death of her grandmother, Geri, who must've beamed a very satisfied smirk that lit up the gates of heaven. Certainly, the newborn filled a void that was created by Geri's death. A new, vivacious life!

I was totally ecstatic as I entered her hospital room ten minutes after she was born. I took her in my arms and felt her little heart pounding rhythmically. The bond was established at that moment, and even now, I feel a special glow whenever I touch her. From the time when she showed some recognition of people who surrounded her, she and I have had that special relationship. Early on, whenever I saw her, she would leave her mother or father and come to me. One of her early utterances was, "Pop-Pop." After starting to walk, she always grabbed Pop-Pop by the fingers and gave him a tour to see things that she had discovered.

For the past two years, from time to time, I have made round-trips from Washington, DC to Frederick, Maryland, to spend time watching her grow and develop. After observing her, I have concluded that she is beautiful and smart, learns fast, and is very cuddly, and because she is my grandbaby, she is the greatest little person in the world; in short, she is now the love of my life. Earlier, I mentioned that my wife, Geri, worked and took charge of our daughters' lives and programs, just as I worked with the boys.

Our other son, Billy, was more interested in working with his hands, so he was always with me when I was building something or making repairs. Some of our hobbies were furniture-making, cabinetry, repairing things on the lawn mower, and making minor automobile repairs, such as brakes, oil changing, parts replacements, and so forth. That's what he enjoyed doing the most. So, when he was over sixteen and in high school, he spent his summers working at auto places such as Jiffy Lube and the Pohanka Automobile Dealership in Virginia. When he went to college, he sold automobiles. After graduating from college, he came back to this area, became a manager of one of the Jiffy Lube franchises, and worked for a couple of years in the DC area. He later transferred to Atlanta to become a regional manager.

After working there for a few years, he realized that the firm was practicing discrimination, so he filed a class-action suit with some other employees and was transferred to a Jiffy Lube affiliate in Houston, Texas. The class-action group went forward with their case and won it. Following the winning of his case, he was hired as a pharmaceutical representative for international company Merck, Inc. He left Houston and went to Charleston, West Virginia, where he bought a house and worked for several years. Still later, he moved to the DC area, worked for Johnson and Johnson, and bought a home in Accokeek, Maryland.

Billy, who had been a most eligible bachelor for a number of years, up to the year 2007, finally met someone whom he felt was the ideal person that he had been seeking for a number of years. Her name is Lisa Pauls, and her immediate family is from the metropolitan Washington area. Ironically, Lisa's mother, a former schoolteacher, was a member of the faculty at Anne Beers Elementary School, where several of my children attended. Mrs. Pauls was one of the kindergarten teachers at Beers and taught Gerald when he was in kindergarten. Lisa's father, Lloyd Pauls, worked at the Library of Congress. They are good, solid citizens who have three children, two girls and one boy.

Billy's wife received her undergraduate degree from Howard University and is also a graduate of the medical school at Howard. She specialized in pediatrics, and currently, she is employed at one of the Kaiser Permanente health care facilities. Presently, I am looking forward to a few more grands, and so, away we go!

CHAPTER XIII

Religion

RELIGION DID NOT BECOME a serious issue with me until I was approximately fifteen years old, and after my involvement in a serious bike accident with an automobile while delivering groceries. All witnesses to the accident and the aftermath swore that I should've been killed. The car rolled over on top of the bike and me, and the only injury that I received was a broken leg, with no other bruises or scratches.

Surviving the crash and subsequent hospitalization and recuperation gave me time to ponder and question the whys of my survival. It was during that period that for some reason unknown to me, it wasn't my time to go and that some power, greater than I, had spared my life. Maybe because I still had a special purpose in life to be fulfilled later!

Less than a year later, I accepted, in the Baptist faith, Jesus Christ as my Lord and Savior. From that day forward, I have accepted the belief that there is a power greater than all mankind who directs my life and all of my endeavors. Throughout life, I have moved with the feeling that everything I do is directed and will come out okay if I listen to my soft inner voice.

In college, I majored in science (biology and chemistry) and later worked in science for more than thirty years; however, nothing that I experienced changed my belief in God as the Supreme Being. If anything, things I saw and experienced while working in science only reinforced my religious beliefs. Science shows an orderliness that bespeaks of a control in and of the universe that even theories are inadequate to explain. Many scientific theories and treatises have been formulated to explain our existence; however, I find them inadequate in explaining all of the phenomena of all of our existence. Probably the most fascinating is living in life itself—be it animal or plant. The fact that we have found only one planet in the whole universe capable of sustaining life, as we know it, gives the crowing touch to God's existence. We tend to revel in our ability to create, but in actuality, nothing is created or destroyed. Everything that we've discovered was already here, waiting to be located and developed. I have learned to accept the fact that the hand of God is everywhere and that we are all God's children. For the aforementioned reasoning, I am able to accept and give full respect to all religious faiths.

CHAPTER XIV

My Wife, the Sensitive 'Schoolmarm' and Ambassador for the Poor and Downtrodden

IT IS SAFE TO say that Geri never worked in a comfortable, middle- to upper-class environment. She started in 1952 in the city of Arlington's hellhole, Green Valley, and proceeded ten years later to the District of Columbia, the dregs of Congress Heights, later toiling for years at Green Elementary School located east of Congress Heights. Following the death of Green's longtime principal, Mr. Randy Jamison, she spent her final years at the Turner Elementary School working with the principal, Mr. Clemmie Strayhorn.

Needless to say, she was a driving force no matter where she went; however, she never felt or had the desire to move away from the areas that needed her type. Her type: the caring and sensitive, the unafraid and the optimist. She always labored under the impression that she could make a difference, and she did. She was also always the type who put her money where her mouth was. After her death, I had the unenviable task of going through the notes, cards, and letters of appreciation from any of her parents, students, and friends whom she had given aid to, financially and otherwise. She was a hands-on person who had no fear of anything or anyone, so she traveled deeply in the bowels of some of the most dangerous areas of southeast DC providing help to the needy. She gave more than her persona; it was everything from fruit baskets at Thanksgiving to food and toys to needy families at Christmas.

She nurtured all of her students and encouraged them to reach for greater heights. Often, students that she mentored proceeded to reach high school and enroll and finish college. She assisted them in applying to colleges and showed them how to get financial aid over and above what she offered them from her personal funds. I learned a lot about her after her passing from Donald Wright, one of her trusted cohorts who was also a distant cousin. He was a long-time custodian (who liked being called an engineer) who worked with her at Green Elementary for a number of years.

She would call on Donald to help her deliver food baskets, clothing, money, and cheer to many of the needy. According to his accounts, he would be shaking in his boots when they entered certain areas of her territories. On none of these trips did Geri show any signs of fear or trepidation. These areas were comprised of drug addicts, winos, pimps, prostitutes, yea, and many needy families. Donald said he was sure that no harm would befall her because many of these people were her ex-students who knew her personally and maybe were her guardian angels as she traveled through these "no trespassing" zones.

For years, she refused to learn to drive on her own. Finally, around 1973, when Valerie was old enough to drive, she purchased a Dodge Swinger, and Valerie became her chauffer. When Valerie went away to college, Mom finally took driving lessons and ventured out on her own. After that, the world was her oyster and hers to roll through anyplace at anytime.

In addition to her professional work, she was a great mother to her family, including me, at times. She became an outstanding cook, and I shared the cooking duties. Whomever came home first prepared the meals. She loved shopping, but as an avid bargain hunter, she never paid full price. She presented gifts for birthdays, Christmas, anniversaries, and many other occasions to both friends and family members.

As a couple, we were like two peas in a pod. If we disagreed, we would find a middle-of-the-road solution and move on. Our children were never aware of any problems between us. They knew that we were of one mind and accord when disciplining them was an issue. We both made sure that all of the needs of our children were met; therefore, one or both of us were always in attendance when one of our children was engaged in any school or community activity. The same action, on our part, was carried out when they went away to college.

My wife, Geri, was the picture of health during approximately forty-plus years following our marriage. The births of the four children and one miscarriage, plus a hysterectomy, were the only breaks she took from her everyday school attendance. After she reached the age of sixty-plus, she began showing some signs of deteriorating health. She never complained, but I was aware of health issues such as high blood pressure, high cholesterol, and a few other minor ailments that she was being treated for by her physicians. She was such a secretive person about her ailments that I often was unaware of her real condition. During the last three or four years of her life, I often accompanied her to her doctors' appointments, but she never revealed any serious conditions that existed, and she never complained. She had the greatest of confidence in all of the doctors who serviced her. Therefore, neither any of the children nor I were aware of the seriousness of her condition until it was probably too late.

For a number of years, we both were served by the same doctor, Dr. Chapman, who was a general practitioner that practiced primarily internal medicine. Upon his retirement, I selected one of his younger contemporaries, and Geri selected another doctor, who was her primary doctor until her death. At one point, she persuaded me to join her and to utilize her doctor as my primary physician. However, I did not like his approach with me as my primary physician. Somehow or another, I had little confidence in him, so I went back to the primary physician,

Dr. Amedeo, that was recommended earlier by Dr. Chapman. Since she was comfortable with her doctor and the service that he provided for her, I stepped aside and made no effort to persuade her to follow me as I made the change.

During the last four years since Geri's death, I've had many hours and days to review in retrospect our more than fifty years together. We had many birthdays, celebrations with our children and grandchildren, anniversaries, graduations, and much more. There were occasions for some sadness, but there was more time when we were overjoyed due to something exciting that happened in our lives. This euphoric ride seemed to be endless, and somehow, we knew it would end, but we never dwelt on that possibility. As I now recall, our last big celebration of an occasion was Geri's fiftieth class reunion at Hampton University in May 2002. The family, as usual, was on hand to help her celebrate. Ironically, it also marked our fiftieth wedding anniversary. Little did I know at the time that this would be our swan song, but it was. I can now say, as I look back, that the sun was setting. We returned home, and for the next nine months, she began to prepare to depart for her permanent home. She began working feverishly on putting her personal records in order. I was always aware that she never discarded letters, documents, or other school papers and magazine articles. Now she was organizing these things in folders with dates and labels. This went on for months prior to her death.

Her final Sunday was spent with Craig, the apple of her eye, as the two of them attended church that morning and were planning to take part in the wedding of one of her dear friends. In addition, she spent the evening with Craig and Melba at Pentagon City Mall in Virginia to help pick out a tuxedo for the wedding, which took place the following Saturday. After they picked the suit, they ate at a restaurant called L&N Seafood, which, needless to say, was Geri's last supper, having it with one of her children and grandchildren that she loved.

The greatest shock of my life came on the morning of Monday, March 31, 2003, at approximately nine o'clock. I was in my office room at home working on the computer when she called out to me. She said in a loud voice, "I have a splitting headache," as she arose from the bed.

I then walked to the master bedroom and asked if she wanted me to take her to the doctor or to the hospital. She replied, "I'm going to take a trip to the bathroom and then decide."

Four or five minutes later, after she had not reappeared, I went to the bathroom, and she was in a semi-prone position on the commode and was unconscious. I spoke to her and touched her but got no response. I immediately went to the front door and saw my neighbor across the street, Ms. Burton, whom I called to come give me a hand with her. She called 911, and within a few minutes, an ambulance was on the scene. They tried to revive her with no success. Promptly, they then prepared her and tried resuscitating her and immediately carried her to the ambulance. We then proceeded to the hospital. My neighbor, Mr. Burton, took me in his car, and we followed the ambulance to the hospital. Ms. Burton stayed in the house and contacted the children. They all came, and we started on a twenty-four-hour vigil during which she was in the intensive-care unit.

During this whole period, it appeared that time stood still. I felt nothing but numbness and a true feeling of powerlessness. Several times, I entered the intensive-care room to see if her condition had changed. Several of the children stood a short distance away and from time to time spoke to her in hopes of seeing some type of response. I also whispered a few words to her and patiently waited for some type of response. Nothing remarkable was seen that would indicate that a spark of life was visible.

During this twenty-four-hour period of intensive care, we all prayed silently for her recovery. We were aware that the doctors and nurses and hospital staff that were in attendance were doing all that they could to affect a recovery. We were apprised by the staff that Geri had suffered a massive stroke due to an aneurysm on the brain. Apparently, a recovery was not to be, and later, we were gathered together with the staff, who indicated that the prognosis was not good.

On the morning of the April 1, they again met with us to explain what efforts had been made in order to determine if there was any hope left for her recovery. We were informed that they had taken special brain scans and used other techniques to determine if there were any brainwaves and had temporarily removed the breathing apparatus to determine whether or not she was breathing on her own. Both of these tests proved to be negative, and, therefore, they suggested that we consider the removal of all life-support systems. Fortunately, several members and two ministers from our church, Pennsylvania Avenue Baptist Church, were there to pray with us and help us in our decision to let her go in peace.

We later were informed by the hospital staff that in order to get a death certificate prepared, an autopsy would have to be performed by the District of Columbia pathologist at the morgue. A day later, I went to the morgue to give a positive identification. The four children got together and divided up the chores necessary for the arrangements of the funeral and interment services. This included the selection of her church as the site for the wake and funeral, the funeral director, and the cemetery where she would be laid to rest. The wake and the funeral were attended by a larger group of people than I have ever seen at these types of events, which was not surprising. This was mainly because of the number of people whom she touched with her services during a half century of service to the communities. She touched the lives of thousands.

I cannot begin to sum up all of her attributes or what she meant to me, and the love we had for each other for more than fifty years. Our marriage vows meant a lot and were carried to finality when death made us part. To that end, I miss her every day of my life. What makes my life continue to be worthwhile is appreciating her legacy. This is to include four beautiful children and the grandchildren, in whom I see an image of her when they are around. I feel that God was good to let her stay in my life for more than fifty years, and blessed be the name of the Lord!

CHAPTER XV

Family Conspiracy from Within

IT HAS BEEN SAID that during the course of one's life, one will always remember the things that created either pleasure or pain. I have looked over my life, and I have experienced both, though not necessarily in equal amounts. I have received a number of awards for many things that were given based on many life accomplishments; however, I would have to classify a certain surprise that was given to me by my family as probably one of the greatest moments in my life.

My immediate family decided among themselves that in my twilight years, I deserved something special. So as a conspiratorial group, they prepared for me a surprise for my seventy-fifth birthday. They quietly contacted many of my relatives and close friends and set the date, time, and location for my most heart-warming affair. The place that it was to be held was the Colony South Hotel in Clinton, Maryland, and it was to include a birthday party, gifts, and a weekend at the hotel at the conclusion of the party.

The person that prepped me for the surprise was my youngest son and top co-conspirator, whose job was to psyche his father. He used a very cunning ploy to set me up. He came to me with a story that one of his friends was purchasing a power boat and had told that friend, who was a coworker, that his father was a polished boater and would be the perfect tutor for him as a mentor on the subject of boating. He told me that they were having a conference at the Colony South Hotel on a Saturday, and we were to meet the guy on November 30 at the hotel to start the mentoring process. He knew I worked every day and often on the weekends at the real-estate office. So, he came by and picked me up, stating that he would drive me to the hotel and bring me back so that I could leave my car at the business office. I fell for the plot, hook, line, and sinker, never thinking about that date being my birthdate, since we never made most of our birthdays as anything special.

We arrived at the hotel and he escorted me to one of the banquet rooms. Arriving in front of the door, I looked back and saw my brother-in-law, Ernest Hooper, and I attempted to yell at Ernie to find out what he was doing there. But before I could utter more than two words, Gerald abruptly ushered me into the banquet room. As I looked in to what was almost semidarkness, there was a huge, thunderous, verbal offering of the "Happy Birthday" song!

What I saw, at a quick glance, was a sea of faces of friends and family members—many of whom I had not seen for a few years. I was totally speechless, which is rare, to say the least, and the rest of the ceremony began to take place. There was much glee, songs, and dancing, and a joyous occasion was experienced by all.

I would have to classify this as probably the most shocking moment of my life—especially after listening to both friends and family members giving speeches on what I meant to them and why. That is an occasion that I will never forget!

You've Seen Dr. Jekyll; Now See Mr. Hyde

One's journey through life is often filled with many moments of happiness, sadness, loneliness, despair, anger, frustration, fear, and other emotions too numerous to describe, but we survive!

I recall in my lifetime at least three times that a situation created in me a period of anger that frightened even me. All of this happened during my childhood and my early youth. The one thing that my parents drummed into me were portions of the Ten Commandments, specifically that one should not bear false witness, cheat, steal, and so forth; therefore, I have practiced those hard and fast rules throughout my life.

Three times during my lifetime, I was victimized in such a way that I was prepared to break one of the most sacred commandments: thou shall not kill. The three incidents were similar: first, I was traveling through Chicago approximately a couple of months after my wedding in Texas. My car trunk was broken into and my wife's clothing, including her most prized possession, her wedding dress, was taken. The second incident was more than thirty years later in Washington, DC, when my wife's car was stolen from in front of our home. It was later recovered after being vandalized.

The third time was when my car was stolen from my driveway as I watched helplessly from my bedroom window. The "clown," at that time, was in the front seat, jimmying the ignition switch, breaking the lock, and hot-wiring the car ignition. By the time I reached the front door, he drove off and was gone. I called the police, which was an effort in futility. They drafted up their stolen-car reports, and that was the last time that I heard from them. The next day, I contacted the insurance company and was told I had to wait out a thirty-day period to see if the car would be recovered by the authorities. It never happened, and consequently, I was paid off for the loss.

Approximately two weeks later, my son Billy located the car at an impound lot; however, it had been stripped of many parts and all of the contents that I had in the car and in the trunk. Needless to say, I made no further move to recover it, since I had been paid by the insurance company.

No doubt, I would have shot to kill the thief, and as I view it today, I would've had no remorse or regrets. The only reason that I did not shoot him was because my gun was not readily available.

I have lived all of my life with the feeling that someone who would break into and enter a person's home or steal properties from a person's home area, is a potential killer, so I plan, even now, to shoot that person and then face whatever the legal consequences are. In all of the cases that I have sighted, I felt very traumatized and personally violated by the incident.

I have resided in Washington, DC, for more than fifty years, and I feel that the gun regulations promulgated and passed as law by the DC government protects only the criminals. However, it doesn't bother me, because when they passed the Gun Control Act in the 1970s, my gun was registered, as required; therefore, subsequent laws allowed people like myself, who owned handguns after the act was passed, to be able to keep their guns using a grandfathered clause, which is a part of the regulations.

The gun regulations that were passed in the 1970s are very asinine in one respect: a burglar feels free and safe to break into a person's home and rob or kill with no fear of being killed or injured. In this city, one feels that the criminals are free to roam the streets while the citizens are jailed in their homes as prisoners with all doors and windows barred. The city officials here remind me of a group of people whose heads are firmly imbedded up their anuses. They don't seem to get it! They don't see that the guns used by the criminal elements come into this city by gun traffickers. Also, most homeowners would not purchase an Uzi or an automatic weapon. The logic of the powers that be is interesting, because their claim is that citizens with guns and houses would provide a source of guns for criminals when their homes are burglarized. Backward-ass logic! My personal feeling is that there will never be cops in my house or near my house to help me at two a.m. when a burglar comes calling. No problem, however, because I will do it myself!

There are a number of reasons why I have concerns about the powers that be and their logic. It starts with the lack of justice in the punishment of first-degree murder cases. The criminals have little fear because they are not going to receive the ultimate punishment, which would be the sacrifice of their lives, due to the idiotic law that outlaws the use of capital punishment (execution). So we continue to spend billions of dollars in the cost of warehousing criminal offenders who don't deserve the air they continue to breathe.

CHAPTER XVI

Race as It's Affected by Politics

THE POLITICAL BALANCE IN the South was set back approximately one hundred years with the Union troops being removed by President Rutherford B. Hayes. In order to win the presidency in his run against Tilden, Hayes promised that if he were elected as president, he would recall all of the Union troops from the Southern states. This was expected to cause a rise of the Ku Klux Klan and other hate groups that would suppress the civil-rights movements of voter registration and the other inherent rights of minority citizens in the South.

From the time of my early youth in Georgia, I realized that being in the heart of Dixie, Negroes were subjected to the controls of only one party: the Democrats. We couldn't vote, so politics were irrelevant and not to be impacted by the Negro race. What intrigued me as I grew up was that no other major political party existed in the South. I learned later that it was only for a short period of time after the Civil War that there was ever any Republican political presence in the South.

I will not dwell on that subject, primarily because history has been well recorded and authenticated by historians relative to the affects that those changes wrought on the Negroes for more than a hundred years; however, I am still intrigued with the attitude of black America relative to party affiliations. What I am presently seeing is that the majority of blacks, both south and north, are willing to be totally bipartisan primarily as Democrats, when we suffered through a full century of indignities by Southern Democrats in the Southern states.

I will not forget the scenes created by Southern "Democratic Demagouges" before, during, and after the civil-rights struggles in the 1950s and 1960s. Therefore, I submit that there is a need for black presence to be seen equally in both major parties. My reason for this type of evaluation is a simple one: as long as we, as a race, favor a single party, the Democrats, they will almost assuredly take our vote for granted. On the other hand, if we refuse to allow ourselves to enter our presence in the Republican Party, their attitude may well be: Since we do not vote in that party, why attempt to curry favors from us? To me, this is basically simple logic.

CHAPTER XVII

Important Issues Facing Men, Women, Young Adults, and Children in the Twenty-First Century

"The stupid logic of same-sex marriage, a
violation of the laws of nature and God"

I MUST CONFESS FROM the outset that I graduated with a degree in biology and worked as a research scientist for more than thirty years. For that reason, I am totally confused with the logic of same-sex involvement and the ultimate goal of same-sex marriage. I am viewing this from the science side as well as the religious side. One of the most fascinating of issues happens to be moral in nature. It seems to be eating away at the very heart and fabric of our nation. It is the acceptance of sexual deviation that has had a death-dealing and devastating affect around the world: homosexuality and AIDS. God, in his infinite wisdom, created man to provide sperm and females to provide eggs in the production of a progeny. We have taken a very cavalier approach to same-sex marriage, which produces no progeny; therefore, my question to my fellow humanoids is this: What is there to be gained when human males have sex with other males or when lesbians cohabitate? In addition, whence comes the next generation from such a union? The answer is: *zilch, zippo,* and *nada,* except physical and psychological satisfaction.

In recent years, I realize that there have been studies conducted where the lower forms of animals attempted to copulate for the purpose of pleasure. Yet still, it has produced no progeny. Our very existence as a human race depends on procreation, which establishes and guarantees future generations. To the best of my knowledge, there has never been an anal birth. So, sperm deposited in the anus would be better dispersed on the earth's surface, where it might help in plant growth. What makes this human behavior so peculiar is that humans, in general, call animals of the field dumb and beastly for the ways in which they behave. However, I have never seen a bull cow mount another bull for the purposes of procreation. If that type of mistake was made, I am certain that once the bull became aware of it, he would dismount, or a hell of a fight would ensue. In all of my study about animals of all kinds and species, human beings present themselves as the most confused of all of the earthly creatures.

I never suspected that I would see the highest-level official in this country, President William J. Clinton, give a new definition to oral sex: when it is performed, it is not a sexual procedure. Following this announcement, laughter could be heard further than from "sea to shining sea" and the world over. The situation even has the religious community totally confused, with all of the confessions and the overt movement called "coming out of the closet." We can only equate what we see relative to why God destroyed Sodom and Gomorrah.

What intrigues me most about this freedom of sexual expression has its roots in the work that was fostered by the civil-rights movement. It apparently has created and unleashed an eight-million-pound gorilla. Even the military created a way to legitimatize homosexuality by saying, "Don't ask, don't tell," or in reality, as the three monkeys pantomimed the illusion: "See no evil, hear no evil, and know no evil."

During the first few months of 2009, the District of Columbia took up the issue on same-sex marriage—not to promulgate legislation relative to the issue of same-sex marriage, but to discuss the issue of DC's concerns about people who were given same-sex marriage legality from other states. This was a preliminary approach to the district considering a position later aimed toward possibly legalizing same-sex marriage in Washington, DC. The counsel was approaching the issue with caution, primarily because of the legal oversight that Congress has over any issues or decisions of interest to the citizens of DC. It was with that in mind that I decided to add my personal opinion by sending a request to the editor of the *Washington Post* to air my opinion. So, here is my opinion, for whatever it is worth: *Washington Post Editor*

May 14, 2009

I am a graduate with a degree in Biology and a research scientist for 30 years. I am totally confused with the insane logic of same-sex marriage. I view this from both science and religion. You would never see a bull mount another bull without the risk of being confused or getting involved in one Hell of a fight. There is nothing to be gained when human males or females attempt to cohabitate with one of the same sex.

God in his infinite wisdom created man to provide sperm and females to provide eggs to produce a progeny. To deal with this illogical act, man is the only animal in the kingdom who utilizes the sex organ for entertainment, while the lower forms of animals use these same organs for procreation. My question to my fellow humanoids: what is there to be gained from this type of sexual involvement, or the ultimate goal: marriage? In addition, whence comes the next generation if this method is in vogue?

W. I. Jones

CHAPTER XVIII

A Message to Today and Future Afro-American Youth

I HAVE LIVED IN Washington, DC, for approximately fifty-seven years and have observed the population in DC and the city leadership go from predominantly Caucasian to predominantly Afro-American. During that time, I have seen the city change from being viewed as a beautiful, sleepy, Southern city to being named "Chocolate City," which currently is the crime capital of the world.

From my first visit in 1942, I viewed some of the biggest crime and crime bosses, who were primarily black, controlling the illegal *Bolito* (lottery-number backers), to the 1970s, when the game became drugs and drug addicts controlled by blacks as it became the new game in town. It was then, after the riots of the late 1960s, when the image of DC was at its worst. As of 2009, the saddest part about the situation in DC is that homicides are more than 95 percent "black on black." Other crimes are equally disproportionate.

I am deeply saddened with the rhetoric coming from the black leaders and the communities with respect to where the black-male brain power is located: in our jails. We want our black male youths to listen to the teaching about the badge of honor worn by former black inmates.

The wisdom prevalent in the black enclave is to let these characters teach our youth because they know all about crime and criminal activity. I would preach the philosophy of crime avoidance as the way to becoming good citizens and good leaders in the communities.

Education was the power that was necessary to remove the chains of slavery and will be the key to unlock the shackles of ignorance. The drive toward the perfection of ignorance seems to be one of the primary goals of our "pied pipers." When I was growing up, we admired the marks of excellence exhibited by our fellow students, whom we lovingly labeled as "eggheads," now called nerds, or in the African nation, Borgie (bourgeoise), or "acting white." They discourage, chide, degrade, and have fun at the expense of the achievers. Until this ignorant, moronic, and destructive philosophy is fleshed from the black community and the new philosophy is instilled, we will continue to be labeled "stupid and ignorant."

There are often grave consequences meted out to people in the African nation who report criminal activity and crime to the police and other authorities. Any type of crime is often tolerated and goes unreported for fear of being labeled a "snitch" or one who is "selling out" his neighbors and friends. Some parents have been benefitting from their kids who deal drugs and peddle stolen goods. Several high-powered drug dealers were cited in several high-profile cases, as reported by members of the DC news media, where parents were participants and recipients of the ill-gained windfalls.

Members of the black nation who don't do drugs or participate in criminal activities are often interested in only sports and entertainment, where little brainpower is required. I must admit that the temptation to pursue these avenues is overwhelming and a lot of money is there for the taking; however, many of the youth with athletic ability and entertaining prowess are ill-educated and unaware of the pitfalls that are lurking in wolf's clothing, interested in taking the suckers inward. They run the gamut from scheming and scamming agents to gold-digging women and drug-dealing leeches.

There are gems that should be what our youth should do as Americans, in the future, to make the country better. My answer is a simple one in that one should let charity begin at home and then spread it abroad. First, start with yourself by looking into the mirror to determine who you are and what you want to be. Among the things to write on a blank sheet are these:

1) To thine own self be true.
2) Show others the way by the example that you set forth.
3) Do unto others as they would do unto you.
4) Let your light so shine that others may see it and glorify your Father, who is in heaven.
5) Do not hide your light under a bush.
6) Be not afraid to go forth to do good.
7) Fear not the critic, when you are doing the right things. (Remember the greatest person who ever lived on this earth, Jesus, who did only his best for all mankind but was crucified for doing good only.)

I often tell my own family, and especially my kids, that I have never seen the inside of a jail or a jail cell. My wife's teaching helped our kids stay out of trouble. I am angered when I realize that many Afro-American families have no concerns about the problems that are created by their children. In fact, often, they encouraged their children, especially when they're engaged in illegal activities that bring money into the family.

CHAPTER XIX

A Historical Update

AFTER A HIATUS OF about four years, from 2006 to 2010, I decided that I needed to update my biography. This was due in part to a few historical changes affecting the African-American populous. We have seen a rise in the number of black coaches in all of the major-league sports (basketball, football, baseball, and many minor-league venues). Our players are showing dominance in all of these sports.

The cream has risen to the top in a few unexpected areas, such as tennis, with the two Williams sisters dominating the tennis circuits over the last few years. They have both won many major tournaments the world over. Several of these tournaments went down to the wire with the finals being a fight to the finish between the two sisters. This guaranteed that the winner would be named Williams.

By all accounts, the most dominant golfer in the last quarter-century is Tiger Woods, who received his early training (from approximately three years of age) from his father, who was a high-level military commander of the army's elite Green Berets and who nurtured this prodigy throughout the early years until he decided to allow professional trainers to take over the honing of the skills of his most prized possession, his son. He hired professionals such as physical trainers and health specialists, including psychologists. He insisted on his son being a

153

college-educated young man; therefore, he was sent to one of the finest schools in the nation, Stanford University, which incidentally has one of the finest golf programs in the world. During Tiger's college career, he won the prestigious world amateur championship three times, which has been accomplished by him only. Finally, over the last ten years or so, he has won major tournaments and is second only in major tournament wins to the greatest hall of famer, Jack Nicklaus. He looks forward to passing Jack in majors won within the next few years.

In the football world, we have had a black football coach, Tony Dungy of the Indianapolis Colts, win the top prize (a Super Bowl championship), with the runner-up, second-place winner being Lovie Smith of the Chicago Bears. What was so unique about this championship was that this was the first time in the history of professional football that both Super Bowl coaches were black—so the foregone conclusion guaranteed that the Super Bowl winning and losing coaches were both African-American. What a thriller!

The basketball world has also seen an increase in the number of African-American coaches over the past few years. We have had a great deal of success from our coaches in the basketball area, with four to five coaches capturing the top prize in professional basketball, starting with such renowned coaches and professional coaches such as Bill Russell, Casey Jones, and a few others.

We are also fielding more baseball managers and coaches. But so far, we have only one World Series winner on our side of the ledger. That one was Cito Gaston of the Toronto Blue Jays, who became the first African-American manager to win a World Series title. African-American athletes have blown away all of the statistics in most of the major sports in which they earn the right to participate. Some of the earliest accomplishments that boggled the minds of sports enthusiasts the world over were the exploits of Joe Louis (world boxing champ from 1936 to 1950); Jesse Owens's mind-blowing achievements in the 1936 track and field Olympiad that embarrassed German Chancellor Adolf Hitler, who refused to shake the hand of that great American athlete;

Alice Coachman, high jumper, who was the first Afro-American woman to win a gold medal in the Olympics; Bill Russell and the Boston Celtics, who won twelve consecutive world championships as professional basketball players; and Hank Aaron, who destroyed the record of the "Great Bambino," Babe Ruth, of 715 home runs in a career.

In professional football, Jim Brown's record still boggles the minds of the football world with his outstanding achievements as probably one of the greatest professional running backs of all time. The first African-American Heisman Trophy winner was Ernie Davis of Syracuse, and Dwight Gooden was the first Cy young Afro-American winner. Jackie Robinson was the first Afro-American major-league baseball player, and Joe Black was the first Afro-American World Series winning pitcher. In tennis, we must not forget two of the African-American giants that paved the way for the Williams girls, and that would be Althea Gibson, the first African-American Wimbledon tennis champion, and Arthur Ashe, the first African-American male Wimbledon champion. One of the first female African-American gymnastic winners to win a gold medal was Dominique Dawes of the 1996 Gymnastic Olympiad.

I am naming just a few of the great hall-of-fame Afro-American sports figures because to do justice to the Afro-American athlete, I would have to write several books and probably would overlook some. Most of these outstanding accomplishments were achieved after the sports bars were lifted approximately sixty years ago.

On the political scene, there has been a sizeable increase in the number of African-American mayors, city councilmen, state and federal representatives, and governors of states; however, our congressional senators still show a single member to climb the twenty-first-century ladder. During my lifetime, I have witnessed a few African-Americans who have had the courage to aspire, as candidates, for the highest-profile position in the world as the president of the United States of America: Sister Shirley Chisolm, Brother Jesse Jackson, and Brother Al Sharpton—all with less than a chance equivalent to that of an unmelted snowball in hell. I must confess that I was less than enthusiastic with those choice candidates as well as with their chances of success. In my humble estimation, none of these candidates were worthy or qualified for the job, but they made history, for what it was worth.

I am probably this cynical because I have lived in Washington, DC, since 1952 and have seen hundreds of politicians come and go from every corner of the continental United States and its territories over that period of time. I have listened to the ranting and raving of some whom I felt were brilliant and highly intellectual and some that were total idiots! Because of the heavy exposure, I have become a very cynical critic who finds it difficult to take most of their dung-type verbiage. Be that as it is, and since I have no other plans or alternatives, I must accept our system. If I had the ability and feasibility to change it, you betcha, I would!

As of 2009, we have had a Republican president for eight years, George W. Bush, with a recent change in the makeup of both houses of Congress, showing a Democratic majority during the last four years, from 2004 to2008. During these years, we have had an inflationary spiral unlike anything that we have had before. The prices on everything has skyrocketed, especially homes. In mid- to late 2007, everything started to spiral downward and out of control. The bottom dropped out of the housing market and banks and other financial institutions began to fail. Numbers of institutions went bankrupt, and homeowners lost homes to mortgage foreclosures. Businesses began to reel, and failures showed up in all entities by the end of 2008.

Near the end of 2007 and throughout all of 2008, there was a political earthquake, the likes of which no one on earth could have ever imagined. To simplify what happened, we will visit the scene: for the first time in our short political history, we launched the presidential campaign of the first serious Afro-American contender for the presidency by the name of Barack Obama, a US senator from Illinois. This was not the first time that an African-American had been placed in position to run as a candidate for the president of the United States of America, but it was the first time that we were able to see a very dim light at the end of the tunnel. We had a more positive feeling because of the qualifications of the Afro-American candidate and his accomplishments as a member of one of the highest branches of the federal government. This was a person who had an impeccable resume, which is always necessary when one is making application for one of the highest positions, not only in the United States, but in the world over.

I will not go into all of the history of Barack leading up the presidential campaign; however, I think it's appropriate to identify his most serious challenger. The challenger was the former First Lady of the White House, Hillary Rodham Clinton, the wife of former president William Jefferson Clinton. None of the major political pundits gave Barack a "Chinaman's chance" to overcome his first major challenger; however, history must record the final results.

For the first time in history, a real grassroots approach was taken, using the Internet as a method of raising campaign funds and exciting the younger and first-time voters to the polls on Election Day. Some of Obama's strongest supporters and campaigners were the students of academia and they dragged along, kicking and screaming, many of their parents and relatives. To the surprise of many people throughout the nation, Obama out-campaigned the established political machinery of Hillary and the traditional Democratic machinery and won the Democratic nomination. Needless to say, he was cast against a true buffoon in the person of the Republican National Committee, the great war hero and true maverick, John Sidney McCain. He immediately solicited the help of one of the most questionably prepared candidates as his running mate, Sarah Palin. As the little known and probably one of the most questionable candidates ever selected as a vice-presidential running mate, the world will little note, but long remember what she did here and what she said here, but they will never forget what little impact she had as a running mate. Suffice it to say that defeat was inevitable, and history will record one of the greatest presidential landslides ever recorded in American history. Therefore, the subject connected with those two losers should not take up any more space in my biography—period!

Before, during, and after the results were reported, Barack Obama was lauded as one of the most serious, intelligent, unflappable, and great speakers since his predecessor, Abraham Lincoln. Generally speaking, he was called the *"Cool Hand Luke"* of the century. After numerous speeches culminating with his inauguration address, almost all persons who listened throughout the campaign and through the inauguration gave him the real kudos that he had earned. One of the things that we do know is that throughout his administration in the presidency, no matter how well he carries himself as the first Afro-American president, he will always have a huge contingent of detractors. Already, he has shown that he plans to surround himself with some of the best and most capable supporters for his administration. I personally have been incensed and angered by the treatment and disrespect orchestrated by many of the ignorant idiots of the Tea Party wing of the Republican Party and the left wing of that party and its supporters. They have developed a propaganda machine second only to Hitler's under his master minister of propaganda, Joseph Von Goebbels. Von Goebbel, a Nazi Reich minister of public enlightenment and propaganda, coined the "Big Lie" technique of propaganda, which is based off the principle that a lie, if audacious enough and repeated enough times, will be believed by the masses. Here are a few white lies tossed out over the airwaves by the Republican goons such as Rush Limbaugh and others: that Obama is not a native and was not born in the United States and that his middle name, Hussein, proves that he is a foreign abstraction and Muslim who owes his allegiance to the Muslims, especially to the Taliban.

Obama, in many of his speeches, including his inaugural speech, has tried to ask for bipartisanship on important issues coming in front of Congress. But on most issues, we still see an extension of the political chaos that caused the Republicans to lose the election. I have watched action in Congress for more than sixty years, living a stone's throw from Capitol Hill, and for the first time, I witnessed a passage of the Healthcare bill in the Senate while the majority of Republicans abstained. This, to me, shows that Jim Crow racist feelings are still running wild, in our so-called "democracy." That is enough about Republican stupidity in my lovely autobiography! Now, let us allow history to run its course.

***

My children are all set for operating and taking care of family matters. Billy has a good job as a pharmaceutical representative, and his wife, Lisa, is a gainfully employed professional pediatrician. Valerie is doing well as a professional photographer and teaching in Prince George's County, Maryland, and her husband Ronald is an attorney employed by the courts in DC. Melba has a very good job as a paralegal with an outstanding company in Columbia, Maryland. Her fiancé, Tommy Sanders, is a supervisor with a creditable and well-known law firm in DC. By the way, they announced their engagement at the third Sunday of August family reunion in 2010.

As the titular head of the Jones family, I have always been supportive of my immediate family, to include spouses of both my sons and daughters. As a successful realtor, I have always been there for them in assisting and advising them in their property investments. Before Gerald married, I helped him secure his first property, a townhouse in Frederick, Maryland. It provided for him an avenue to clear his indebtedness prior to his marriage. Candy, his wife, was the recipient of that investment after they were married and when he placed her name on the title of that property. They lived there for a few months after marriage and sold the townhouse at approximately $150,000. That allowed them to move to an upscale, detached home valued at more than a half million dollars. As their agent, I helped in the contract negotiations. I also helped Gerald to purchase an investment property that he sold in less than six months in which he netted more than $30,000. The only child that I have who is currently battling with a costly problem is Gerald. His marriage fell apart in 2007 through no fault of his own. He was dragged through a very messy divorce, which almost carried him into bankruptcy. Helping him save his home and get through this major crisis with lawyer and court fees and other incidentals created a soul-searching decision on my part on his behalf.

Fortunately, I found a way to resolve the issue by creating a way to clear the financial crisis. Since my home was owned free and clear, I decided to do a reverse mortgage and take out enough to save Gerald's home. This, I knew, would make it possible to save his home and provide a place for him to live in comfort and to be prepared to raise his daughter—my youngest, beautiful granddaughter.

His ex-wife was not prepared for the action and the results ministered by the courts and the protection I provided for my son and ultimately for my grandchild. She thought that she was going to receive a large sum if she forced the sale of the house. The "old fox" that I am knew what to do with my nearly thirty years of real-estate experience, and the house did not have to be sold, which would have left Gerald and Gabby without a home. Gerald spent nearly ten years trying to overcome the disaster, and it has taken a toll, but I feel he will overcome it and continue to make preparations for his daughter's future and his new life. My daily prayer is the hope for my granddaughter's sake that she has a long and successful life.

I am writing this saga in my life to clarify the actions I felt compelled to take in my estate will to rectify the family situation—as I must do to ensure that none of my family members feel slighted based on my decision. I will do, as always, my best to treat all fairly as I view the action I am taking.

I had to take out the reverse mortgage of my home to help Gerald defray the cost of his attorney fees. I placed approximately $200,000 into the house, causing me to become part owner, so that his note is low enough to afford to live decently with Gabby and help with her future, which may not be properly secured.

Gerald lost his job in the early part of 2010, so I had to rescue him as his sole supporter.

The reverse mortgage is to be paid on an installment basis until I pass away or the note is paid off completely, or if the house is sold. Presently, since no payment on the note is being made and is not required to be made, it is due after I'm gone or if the property is sold. It is an FHA-type loan, as all reverse mortgages are. Wells Fargo is a loan financial institution. The loan company will explain the necessary details.

The money that I provided for Gerald's home, approximately $180,000, lowered Gerald's note to approximately $260,000. That allowed me to have about a one-half share interest in the property. This allowed him to live there and pay the note until it is paid off. The estimated value of the property as of November 2010 is approximately $530,000. So my one-half share interest of the estate property will be addressed in my will and testament.

Interest is being accrued on the reverse mortgage, and some time in the future, pending my longevity, the mortgage on the home may exceed the market value, but that is allowed to happen on a reverse mortgage. That note is to be addressed or dealt with only if the owner passes or if the property is sold. One option available, when it becomes estate property, is to rent it to maintain it as a family estate by paying a monthly note, to sell it, or, heaven forbid, allow it to become a foreclosure. The choice will be made by my heirs: Valerie Thomas, Melba Sanders, Bill Jones Jr., and Gerald Jones.

Health Care or What?

What we know about or have available to us in the year 2010 was near nonexistent for most of the nation's poor and underprivileged as I grew up in Georgia in the 1930s and early '40s. In the first place, there were a limited number of Afro-American doctors in my hometown. They had no access to the hospital for treatment of their patients, as hospitalization was only on an emergency basis. Surgery was performed on Afro-Americans only by white surgeons who had unlimited use of the hospital facilities.

The hospital in my hometown of Albany, Georgia, was the Phoebe Putney Memorial Hospital. There was a six-bed ward for Negro males, and I never knew how Negro women were served. The reason that I knew about the male ward was because I was in an auto-bicycle accident on November 30, 1939, and had a broken right thigh-bone (above the knee) and stayed in the hospital for two weeks. The delivery of baby Negroes was done at home by midwives, for the most part.

All the school-age kids entering elementary school were required to have vaccinations for measles and smallpox. Mumps was expected to be handled in a different manner. It was expected and often treated at home by some crude methods. The young children were intentionally exposed to mumps and were allowed to get the disease through contact. This exposure ostensibly set up a life-long immunity for the person once having had the disease. Most of the illnesses we encountered were of short duration and were cured by the old-fashioned remedies.

My first real awareness of medical treatment in a modern, professional way came about by one of life's general circumstances: I was inducted in the military during WWII, signed in the navy and became a medical-aid corpsman, where I studied and worked for approximately two years. Soon after leaving the navy and entered Hampton as a pre-med student, I became completely sensitized to the need for health-care maintenance from birth to death.

Both my wife, Geri, and I started medical-maintenance programs soon after we married. We selected a primary-care physician and went to specialists when necessary. When our children were born, all in hospitals using strict medical procedures, they were assigned to pediatric care until they reached adulthood. All of the preventive medical practices were carried out, which also included dental care.

Only one of our children had an operation in his early years. Gerald, our youngest, had an operation for a hernia at a year old, and the surgery was successful. At an early age between his junior and senior years in high school, we discovered Gerald had a condition called scoliosis, a minor curvature of the spine. For a few years, he used a special medical device called a scoliotron to correct the curvature. This does not provide a complete cure, but it may prevent a major deformity.

After growing up to adulthood, only a few operations had been performed on my children and my wife and I. I had a major surgical operation on my lower spine in 1979/1980. It was a spinal-disc operation that was done, and for more than thirty years, I have had no problems connected with any spinal condition. In my agency, the FDA, I was fortunate to be in a random selection of employees of forty years old and over who were placed in a medical-monitoring program for major screening checkups every two years. After retiring, I contracted type-II diabetes, which is now controlled by medication. I had a minor stroke in 1999, but no minor or major paralysis has ever been observed. Between 2008 and 2010, I've had bouts of vertigo, but it soon passes. At eighty-five years old, I still live alone, drive where I need to go, and enjoy my family, especially the grandkids!

Two of my children, Melba and Billy, have been operated on successfully for the removal of their gallbladders with no signs of after-effects. In addition, Melba had a successful appendectomy in 1997 with no after-effects.

All of the grandchildren have been healthy: Craig of twenty-seven years to Ronnie of twenty-three years, Kyra of eighteen years and Gabby of ten, with one exception. When Gabby was three years old, she had her tonsils and adenoids removed. She has shown no adverse effects. Family illnesses of note that I'm aware of show my mother with very few problems until she was over eighty years old. She had a few hospital runs, but nothing of lasting effect. She contracted diabetes and used insulin after reaching eighty years of age, and she expired later of natural causes four months shy of her 101st birthday. My father was the picture of health until he was about sixty-three years of age, when he became a diabetic and lost both legs and part of his thighs after a few operations. He later passed in 1976. At best, we never knew his official age, and we felt that he was born in approximately 1894.

Overall, as a family, we never had to be overly concerned about health-care coverage of the cost of our medical needs. The reason that we never had to worry about it was because I worked for the federal government and had health-insurance coverage for the family, and Geri worked for the District of Columbia government as a professional teacher and assistant principal, jobs that also had adequate health-maintenance insurance policies.

CHAPTER XX

The Continuation of the Hampton Legacy

AFTER A HIATUS OF approximately two decades, the engine driving the family Hampton tradition was restoked with the entry of my first grandson, Craig Stafford II, in the freshman class at Hampton University in September 2006. It was a very exciting time to get started again to extend the dreams of the departed matriarch, Geri, who, before her death, dreamed of Craig carrying the torch forward. Craig's mother, Melba, and I could not rest easily until Craig's entry into Hampton. Watching him pass through his final four years at High Point High School in Beltsville, Maryland, we always felt comfortable that he intended to honor his beloved grandmother's dreams and continue the family legacy.

The whole Jones family supported Craig during the four years that he matriculated at Hampton by attending all of the homecomings and many of the major functions that Craig was involved in. There were never any indications that we noticed that Craig would ever fail to carry out his end of the contract, and he appeared to be enthusiastic about his work and his participation in many of the extracurricular activities that the campus provided for its students. For example, in his freshman year, he was involved in student government as a chief of staff to the president of the SGA and was a member of his freshman executive council that supports class activities for the freshmen. During his sophomore year, he continued to work with the student government to raise more funds for student activities during the 2007–2008 school year and was instrumental in the student government Senate committee in working to develop academic, financial, and registration proposals that recommended solutions to problems in those areas that benefitted the student body. In addition, Craig also participated in a municipal campaign, canvassing in the Hampton Roads area to help elect state senators and representatives. A year later, in his junior year, he not only participated in campus and municipal affairs but also became involved in one of the most important national political issues facing Hampton University and the nation: the presidential election of 2008.

During Craig's junior year, as a newly elected president of the Political Science Club, a member of the Young Democrats of America, and a veteran member of the Student Government Association, he worked with the Hampton chapter of the Democratic Convention to register the student body to vote for the upcoming election, where they were successful at registering more than a thousand students on the campus. What was intriguing about this process was not just the quantity of students who were participating in the campaign and getting registered, but the quality of the plan to register the students in the state of Virginia.

Given the overwhelming population of students who were from areas such as Maryland, the District of Columbia, New York, and California, primarily many of them were from democratically held states, which would not help the chances of Obama winning traditionally Republican "red" states. So, their plan was to register students in the state of Virginia, which was a "swing" state, and increase the chances of Obama's win for the electoral votes of that state. The plan worked, and Virginia, for the first time in approximately forty years, went "blue" for the 2008 presidency.

Craig's senior year at Hampton brought on the dawn of another day. It was the successful culmination of several events, one of which was the election of Barack Obama as the president of the United States. Craig then turned his attention to completing the marathon race of his life to graduate from college. It was during this last year that he began to concentrate on his future, which would be the beginning of his career. He determined that out of all of the fields of endeavor that were available to him, he needed to concentrate his efforts toward the next step in the development of a career. His major was political science, and he quickly viewed the federal government as a potential source in which to enter in helping to develop his career.

Since he majored in political science and concentrated in the German and Russian languages and had the experience of being cursorily involved in the presidential campaign, he decided that with his background, maybe a career in the foreign service would not only be interesting but also an educational venture. Therefore, upon his graduation, he applied to several universities in order to further his direction toward the foreign service. To that end, he accepted the offer at Johns Hopkins University to seek an advanced degree in strategic studies, later getting his master of science degree in security studies at the University of Maryland in security studies.

During the weekend of May 9, 2010, I enjoyed one of the most exciting times of my life at my alma mater; the *real* HU, Hampton University. Fifty-nine years after my graduation, I, along with many of the emeritus class members, was there to personally view a history that we could never have envisioned. We were visiting our alma mater during its finest hour. Hampton was the first historically black college in the United States, founded by a Union general, Samuel Chapman Armstrong; a place where the Emancipation Proclamation was read under the old oak tree that still stands; the alma mater of Booker T. Washington; and a place where three US presidents (William H. Taft, George H. W. Bush, and the first African-American US president, Barack H. Obama) had visited and spoken on special occasions.

Significantly, most of the world leaders look to President Obama to give new direction to a troubled world. He also received the Nobel Peace Prize, which was the first time such an honor has been bestowed upon a sitting president of the United States.

During that weekend, it was historical to see President Obama speak to Craig's class during the graduation commencement. It was truly something that I could never have envisioned growing up in the segregated South. My proudest moment during the commencement was watching my first grandchild, Craig, receiving his bachelor of arts degree at the convocation center on the campus. I shed no tears, but I lost all of the buttons on my shirt due to my swollen chest. His graduation meant that he was carrying on a tradition started by Geri and I, his mother and father, two uncles and aunt, and several cousins.

I also received a call from my second grandson, Ron Thomas, saying that the tradition was not going to be broken, as he had been accepted to matriculate at Hampton University for the fall of 2010. He had been on the fence until he attended Craig's graduation. He was impressed by President Obama's speech, and he also became aware that the Hampton University president, William R. Harvey, was appointed by President Obama to chair the president's Board of Advisors on Historically Black Colleges and Universities. In 2014, Ronnie completed his bachelor's degree in Marketing at Hampton, and later, he plans to earn his master's degree.

Shortly after Craig graduated from college, he, like most post-graduates, was looking to enter the workforce. In a country that faced the biggest recession since the Great Depression and a scarce job market, the class of 2010 faced many challenges finding work, especially in the careers they dreamed of attaining. Craig took the initiative to not only apply to job announcements on the Internet; he also sacrificed his free time to travel distances to meet with employers who were willing to bring in a new generation of young talent and professionalism.

Craig had held two retail jobs and a voluntary internship with a nongovernmental organization the summer after his graduation, but he kept on applying until he had found a solid footing that was more conducive to his career goals. After five months of networking and cold-contacting employers, in October 2010, he was selected for a position at the US Department of State as a paid intern under the Student Temporary Employment Program (STEP) in the Bureau of Human Resources. He was processing employment applications for civil- and foreign-service applicants, to include the student-internship program applications. The internship program Craig was part of provided the opportunity that upon graduation, he would be non-competitively converted to a civil-service employee with full-time, permanent status.

Not only did Craig get a job while also working on his master's degree; he was also provided with access to the world's most oldest and well-respected department—the foreign arm of the United States government, where he can develop a career in the US Foreign Service. Since his time at the State Department, he had applied to another vacancy and was accepted for a position as a management analyst at the Office of Inspector General (OIG) in the Security and Intelligence Division. He has traveled to several countries in Europe, the Middle East and South America for his job assignments and continues to advance in his federal career. Over the years, Craig has excelled in his career, where he has received new opportunities within the State Department. After doing two short years in the OIG, he received a rotational opportunity working on counterterrorism in Africa and the Middle East. After he graduated, his boss converted his internship assignment to a full-time permanent position, where he then received his federal tenure as a foreign-affairs officer working on cyber-policy.

One of the most interesting things I noticed about Craig over the years was not only his seasoned networking and career-mobility skills that he utilized to advance in his junior career, but the fact that he was also able to get promoted each year along the way. After starting out as a GS-05, he attained the rank of a GS-12 in just under five years—which took me nearly thirty years to get. I expect nothing but great things from this young man and a prosperous future in every walk of life.

CHAPTER XXI

Poverty, Protest, Progress, and Prosperity

Poverty

During the writing of my bio, describing my poverty has been easy. It was having the bare minimum of necessities to exist (i.e., food, clothing, and shelter). At that time, my family was living in what was known as a modern society, but without running water, adequate sanitation facilities, updated lighting, and transportation. These things were available in the land of the free and the home of the brave in the richest country in the world, yet these things were out of reach for the local, tired, and depressed masses, and the conditions were totally unacceptable.

The irony that we, the raggedy masses, viewed was watching immigrants from foreign countries arriving in our country, where we shared blood with the rest of the endogenous Americans and yet had few freedoms. If they had money, they were free to go into any hotel, park, or theater and board trains, buses, or any other public service available without fear of being bounced and/or jailed like we would've been. They also could be trained to do white-collar work or highly skilled jobs, technical work, and so forth, and they were hired, but we weren't.

Protest

In the 1960s and 1970s, people thought they were protest pioneers; however, if they studied history, they would see that over the years, protesters have used numerous strategies and stages to accomplish their missions. For example, Marion Anderson, one of the greatest singers of all times, performed at the Lincoln Memorial in 1939, and she was not allowed to sing at Constitution Hall in Washington, DC, which was owned by the Daughters of the American Revolution (DAR). An individual protest was launched by a bus rider named Rosa Parks in Montgomery, Alabama, in 1955. In addition, no one can forget the protest of two athletes, Tommy Smith and John Carlos, in Mexico City at the Olympic Games awards ceremony, showing their opposition to the continued suppression of blacks in the United States.

Martin Luther King's pioneer movement of large groups marching together to emphasize the need for change was a brilliant, masterful position using mass protest. King used this process in a number of cities to arouse the public over massive acts of segregation and discrimination throughout the United States, but more overtly in the South. He touched the conscience of the majority of Americans as they began to be aware of the lie perpetrated over the years in the so-called "land of the free," that all persons are created equal. Other than the march on Washington, he also had majority activities in Selma and Birmingham, Alabama; Memphis, Tennessee; Atlanta, Georgia; Cairo, Illinois; and several other locations.

There were other small groups who performed other activities, such as sit-in demonstrations, in states like North Carolina, primarily at restaurants and lunch counters in drugstores. Many people of different races and religious groups were aroused and took part even when groups such as the KKK, city police, sheriffs, and governors of states and hate groups threatened them with legal action or violence, bodily harm, and death.

Many African-Americans were unable to participate for a number of legitimate reasons; however, they stood on the sidelines and cheered for the brave heroes who ran the gauntlet, knowing that death might be at the end of the line, as it was for Dr. King, Emmet Till, and children bombed in churches, just to cite a few. All were great heroes that are admired by those of us who are the recipients of their courageous efforts and bravery. Those of us who survived and benefitted from those who gave their supreme sacrifice have not stood idly by. We had to continue the war, often in silence, with heads bloodied but unbowed.

There were a lot of jobs to be performed after we buried our dead. We had to desegregate schools and housing, and prepare to fight for technical and scientific jobs. Those who were victims of systems that required new grounds to be cultivated (e.g., equal employment and housing covenants to be eliminated) above all, we know that we are not there yet.

My protest came with no malice or forethought. We had been awakened by hate groups such as the Ku Klux Klan, the Daughters of the American Revolution, and others who were trying to prevent us from gaining our freedom. These groups swung into action (*"to keep the niggers in their places"*). So when they saw massive peaceful protests by us, they donned their white, pinheaded robes and went to war. They openly started stirring up these hate groups to maim, brutalize, and even kill any participants who were in the act of gaining freedom. This action required them to openly disrupt any freedom movement that they observed. It was total war! With training in the use of guns, bats, water hoses and bombs, these weapons were used on the protest groups. They hoped that ultimately, these types of pressures would cause the groups to disband and go back to being ex-slaves.

I believed that my feelings about protest did not fit in with the philosophical approaches laid out by the mass-approach method. One of the reasons was that I felt that the majority of the protesters were conditioned to accept some of the human behaviors that ensued during large protests. I could not accept the Martin Luther King/Mahatma

Ghandi philosophy of nonviolence, because I personally would not sit or stand and allow eggs or saliva to be thrown in my face without taking personal action. That is why I chose to act as an individual, doing things my way instead of following the masses. During these demonstrations, I took the silent approach, which called for working with individuals and small groups to accomplish my goals in a small arena that would change the attitudes of the white majority that I encountered. To that end, I envisioned that my effort would have an impact on a small group that needed to see a different approach.

Progress of the Black Masses

My individual progress was initiated primarily after my graduation from Hampton Institute. The first move was initiated because after graduation, I was unable to find work in the field that I had selected for my future. Therefore, with no other choice, I decided to go into the military for a couple of years to allow me to analyze a situation relative to employment available to African-Americans. I was already aware that the country had not arrived at the era of a national concern connected with equal employment opportunity. The situation of fairness to African-American servicemen was only a little better than what was seen in the private sector. Changes within the military were initiated around the period of the 1950s. I was engaged in the conversion of several military units when the order came down from headquarters.

Approximately a year later, in the military (c. 1953), I decided that it was time to take my leave from the military to see what civilian life would provide for my future. One of the reasons for that decision was based on the fact that I was now married, and my wife was working in the school system of Virginia. I did not like the idea of being in the military and attempting to rear a family. When I arrived in the metropolitan Washington area, I decided that a career in the federal government would help to stabilize my life, liberty, and pursuit of happiness.

The foundation for progress was laid as the secession of World War II. Many African-American men came home and were able to get degrees in higher education. We then could qualify for higher-paying jobs. Also, America really turned its power, and the country moved toward a new, great industrial revolution. We still had work to do and needed laws and legal support. We delved deep into the legal system to provide laws with teeth. The desegregation of schools was the primary movement that gave rise to other movements, such as fair housing and equal-employment laws. Fair-housing laws were established that worked. These became more effective laws when the African-American real-estate agent began to be hired by major realtor companies. These agents made the system work in fair housing because the black clients could view homes that were outside the ghetto areas. It took awhile to get the process to work effectively. It has taken decades, but now we have the ball rolling. We have to be vigilant to keep in touch to continue progress.

Prosperity

Prosperity shows many facets. Primarily, we consider that we have prosperity when we are able to buy decent homes, get the best education for our offspring, purchase luxurious items such as beach homes, yachts, luxury automobiles, decent clothing, and food items of our choice. It also includes establishing a decent savings account, being able to have a night out and take vacations now and then and to entertain our guests, and beyond that, to be able to live comfortably and cover ourselves so that we are comfortable in our homes as we age. Prosperity changes with time, and the ultimate prosperity is to be able to enjoy the creature comforts that have been advanced by technology.

Sports during the decades of my life have provided many of our athletes with a way out of the ghetto. The arena that we traveled to prosperity were baseball, basketball, football—and to a limited degree—boxing. Our athletes were able to make football and basketball a two-edged sword for several decades. They matriculated at many of the top colleges that provided a platform that allowed them to get educated, as well as having an instant, well-paying job in sports.

The military life served by many of our servicemen, helped to establish the mid-income level after the cessation of the war. This generation of young men during the mid-40s and early 50s were drafted for service, for the duration of the war in 6 months total. The ex-servicemen who entered colleges got their tuitions, room and board and all supplies and educational equipment (e.g. books, other school supplies, etc.) based on the need of the courses. In addition, we received a stipend of $100 per month for other uses.

Upon completion of my four years of college, I found that jobs were scarce, but since I took a course in military science and tactics, I entered the Army and stayed until the economy took a turn for the better. Entering the Food and Drug Administration as a scientist provided me with a ladder to climb to prosperity. It was very shaky at times, but I clung to it to provide for a way for my children and grandchildren, so that they too could reach the Promised Land—prosperity.

MY SPORTS HALL OF FAME

1) Baseball
    a) Jackie Robinson – Second Baseman
    b) Larry Doby – Outfielder
    c) Don Newcombe – Pitcher
    d) Joe Black – Pitcher
    e) Fergie Jenkins – Pitcher (six consecutive twenty-game seasons)
    f) Roy Campanella – Catcher
    g) LeRoy "Satchel" Page – Pitcher

2) Boxing
    a) Joe Louis
    b) Sugar Ray Robinson
    c) Henry Armstrong

3) Basketball
    a) Bill Russell
    b) Wilt Chamberlin
    c) K. C. Jones
    d) Red Auerbach (coach)
    e) Kobe Bryant

4) Football
    a) Jim Brown
    b) Jerry Rice

5) Track and field:
    a) Jessie Owens
    b) Ralph Metcalf
    c) Carl Lewis
    d) Marion Jones
    e) Florence Joyner
    f) Alice Coachman
    g) Michael Johnson

6) Tennis
    a) Arthur Ashe
    b) Althea Gibson
    c) Serena Williams
    d) Venus Williams
    e) Pete Sampras
    f) Poncho Gonzales

7) Bowlers
    a) Gerald Jones
    b) William "Billy" Jones
    c) Craig Stafford II
    d) Valerie Thomas

I will always be enthralled by my top three picks for my hall of fame, whose first initials are *J, J,* and *J*: Joe Louis, Jesse Owens, and Jackie Robinson. They are my top three picks because they all were groundbreaking pioneers. They paved the way for black athletes during a period when we were not accepted as being worthy to compete against white athletes. In addition, my second group of great pioneers in sports have the first initials *A, A,* and *A*: Alice Coachman, Althea Gibson, and

Arthur Ashe. They all shattered the barriers and opened the door for our inclusion in the world of professional sports.

In each case, they were exposed on a world stage and proved that we belonged here. The 1936 Olympiad insult in Germany, when Hitler refused to show sportsmanship and respect to Owens, who was the greatest black athlete and won multiple gold medals at that special track meet, showed how great black athletes were who made the United States look mighty in athletics. In return, these great athletes would receive almost no respect and appreciation from whites for their contribution to athletics and entertainment. History is loaded with all of the superlatives about my top-three J athletes; however, my special accolades belong to Joe Louis and Jesse, because they both destroyed Hitler's myth about his "Aryan race of blond," Caucasian superiority.

One may see that in my hall of fame select, I have chosen not only great performers in the field of athletics; these were also gentlemen and ladies with character who earned the respect of other nations. They were humble, honest, upstanding citizens whom we could be proud to know.

PHILOSOPHY OF LIFE

My favorite bible quote: Psalm 23, A Psalm of David

> *The LORD [is] my shepherd; I shall not want.*
> *He maketh me to lie down in green pastures: he leadeth me*
> *beside the still waters.*
> *He restoreth my soul:*
> *he leadeth me in the paths of righteousness for his name's sake.*
> *Yea, though I walk through the valley of the shadow of death,*
> *I will fear no evil: for thou [art] with me; thy rod and thy*
> *staff they comfort me.*
> *Thou preparest a table before me in the presence of mine enemies:*
> *thou anointest my head with oil; my cup runneth over.*
> *Surely goodness and mercy shall follow me all the days of*
> *my life:*
> *and I will dwell in the house of the LORD for ever.*

My favorite religious song, "Just a Closer Walk with Thee"[1]

> *I am weak, but Thou art strong;*
> *Jesus, keep me from all wrong;*
> *I'll be satisfied as long*
> *As I walk, let me walk close to Thee.*

Refrain:
Just a closer walk with Thee,
Grant it, Jesus, is my plea,
Daily walking close to Thee,
Let it be, dear Lord, let it be.

Through this world of toil and snares,
If I falter, Lord, who cares?
Who with me my burden shares?
None but Thee, dear Lord, none but Thee.

When my feeble life is o'er,
Time for me will be no more;
Guide me gently, safely o'er
To Thy kingdom shore, to Thy shore.

My greatest poem of wisdom, the Serenity Prayer by Reinhold Niebuhr

"God grant me the serenity to accept the things I cannot change;
courage to change the things I can; and wisdom to know the difference."

My favorite poem, "Thantatopsis" by William Cullen Bryant

So live, that when thy summons comes to join
The innumerable caravan, which moves
To that mysterious realm, where each shall take
His chamber in the silent halls of death,
Thou goeth not, like the quarry-slave at night,
Scourged to his dungeon, but, sustained and soothed
By an unfaltering trust, approach thy grave
Like one who wraps the drapery of his couch
About him, and lies down to pleasant dreams.

My favorite orators
- President Abraham Lincoln
- Dr. Martin Luther King, Jr.
- President Barack Obama

My favorite singers

Classical
- Marion Anderson
- Leontyne Price
- Todd Duncan
- Paul Robison

Jazz

- Billy Eckstein
- Ella Fitzgerald
- Sara Vaughn
- Diana Washington
- Arthur Prysock
- Joe Williams
- Jimmy Rushing

My favorite musicians

Jazz saxophonists
- Ben Webster
- Illinois Jacquet
- Lester Young

Trumpeters
- Gerald Jones
- Louis Armstrong
- Dizzie Gillespie
- Erskine Hawkins

- Cootie Williams

Vibraphone
- Lionel Hampton

Pianists
- Duke Ellington
- Count Basie
- Milt Jackson

Jazz organist
- "Wild Bill" Davis

Drummers
- Lionel Hampton
- Joe Jones

Guitarist
- Wes Montgomery

My Favorite Political Figures

Presidents
- Abraham Lincoln (for the emancipation of slaves)
- Franklin D. Roosevelt (cured Depression ills and set the stage for winning World War II)
- Harry S. Truman (closed out World War II and began the desegregation of the US military)
- John F. Kennedy (For standing down Russian president Nikita Khrushchev and continuing efforts to resolve civil-rights issues)
- Lyndon B. Johnson (for expanding the fight initiated by John F. Kennedy and Robert F. Kennedy)
- President Barack Obama

Mayors

- Walter Washington, Washington, DC
- Anthony Williams, Washington, DC

Judges

- Thurgood Marshall (for his integral role in arguing civil-rights cases before he became member of the Supreme Court)
- Chief Justice Warren

College and university presidents

- Samuel Chapman Armstrong (founder of Hampton Institute)
- Booker T. Washington (most famous of all Hampton Institute alumnus, primarily because he founded Tuskegee Institute, which hired and supported G. W. Carver)
- William R. Harvey (current president of Hampton University, starting his term in March 1979, is the best and most qualified president ever employed by Hampton Institute and University. He is such an innovative, resourceful, and respectful individual.)
- Joseph W. Holley (founder of Albany State University)

Scientists

- G. W. Carver (greatest of all scientists in the United States! He developed more useful products from his research in plants that benefited humanity than any other scientists.)

The cars that I have owned:

1. 1950 Dodge Wayfarer Convertible
2. 1953 Dodge Coronet
3. 1955 Dodge Custom Royal Lancer
4. 1960 Dodge Polara
5. 1967 Dodge Monaco
6. 1972 Dodge Monaco
7. 1979 Chrysler Fifth Avenue

8. 1984 Chrysler Fifth Avenue
9. 1989 Chrysler New Yorker
10. 1996 Chrysler LHS
11. 2005 Chrysler 300C

My favorite mottos

"If a task is once begun, never leave it until it's done. Be
the labor, great or small, do it well or not at all."
–Author unknown

"You can make it, if you try."

"You can knock me down, but stand over me; you'll have to do it again."

"All is well that ends well."

"I ask no one to give me respect. I expect to earn it,
and if I earn it, no one can take it away."
–William I. Jones

"The fact that I have lived through nine decades, I have not
only studied and retained history; I am history!"
–William I. Jones

ENDNOTES

[1] http://www.metrolyrics.com/just-a-closer-walk-with-thee-lyrics-tammy-wynette.html

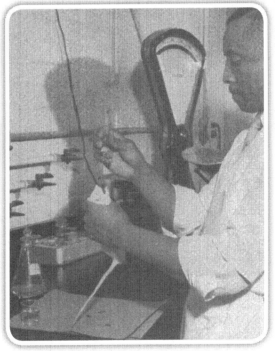

204

207

Made in the USA
Lexington, KY
14 January 2016